GRAVE

EXPECTATIONS

Planning the end like there's no tomorrow

by Sue Bailey & Carmen Flowers

CIDER MILL PRESS

BOOK PUBLISHERS

KENNEBUNKPORT, MAINE

HOMEWOOD PUBLIC LIBRARY

JUL - - 2010

13-Digit ISBN: 978-1-60433-021-2
10-Digit ISBN: 1-60433-021-X

This book may be ordered by mail from the publisher. Please include $3.50 for postage and handling. Please support your local bookseller first!

Books published by Cider Mill Press Book Publishers are available at special discounts for bulk purchases in the United States by corporations, institutions, and other organizations. For more information, please contact the publisher.

Cider Mill Press Book Publishers
"Where good books are ready for press"
12 Port Farm Road, Kennebunkport, Maine 04046

Visit us on the web!
www.cidermillpress.com

Design by Jessica Disbrow Talley
Printed in China

1 2 3 4 5 6 7 8 9 0
First Edition

TABLE OF CONTENTS

DEATH MAY BE THE GREATEST OF ALL HUMAN BLESSINGS.

— *Socrates*

We sat in the church with our mouths wide open, wondering if we were in the wrong place. The person the preacher was talking about was not our friend. Why do so many people try to sanctify someone when they die, instead of honoring and celebrating their personality and life? We wanted the man who drank too much, left his family for weeks on end, and went through a journey that brought him back to his family and friends a whole person. His true story had courage.

It was on the drive home from that funeral that we began to toy with the idea of writing this book. Once we got home and drank enough champagne, we made the commitment to write it.

Life is such a rich, complicated, joyous, mysterious, wild ride. Everyone has stories to tell and lessons to pass on, and what better way to do that than when you're dead? It was your life; your funeral is the one time you should do and say absolutely whatever you want.

Were you reluctant to pick up this book? Have you been dreaming of a royal, pull-out-all-the-stops funeral like Princess Diana had? Or perhaps in lieu of a formal funeral, would you rather send your closest friends to a sexy tropical island to celebrate your life? Would you like to have a lovely, tasteful tribute to yourself that includes your joys, sorrows, triumphs—and yes, some mistakes? Are you worried that your family will be embarrassed by your end-of-life festivities plans that include sending your ashes up in a space capsule? Would you be mortified if they want to embalm you and put you in a huge, metal casket with your internal organs lying right next to your legs? If you answered "yes" to any of these questions or have other ones . . . this is the book for you.

As of this writing, there is no alternative to dying. (You can be cryogenically frozen, but we wouldn't call that life.) Since there's no getting out of it, why not go ahead and plan your fantasy "going away" party? Is it just us or have you been seeing too many "She's not dead, she's just away" bereavement cards? Of course you can't really be too upset, since according to the card, she's coming back.

We were destined to write a book about planning one's own funeral. Between us, we've personally experienced three weddings, two divorces (all Carmen), and five suicides of close family members. We've nursed four relatives and friends through deaths due to cancer. We've survived cancer (Sue) and meningitis (Carmen), and if all that's not enough, we are both orphans. In spite of these experiences, or because of them, we do not fear death at all. In fact, we appreciate life that much more.

In the midst of our writing this book, Carmen's godmother, Didi—the woman who raised her—died. There is one bright side to this otherwise sad occurence—Didi had written down her wishes in an early draft of this book, which gave her goddaughter and relatives an easy-to-follow "funeral map." Didi had chosen the church, the liturgy, the friends and family she wanted to speak at the service, and in some cases, the topics they would address. She was an artist, and she had chosen the various drawings, illustrations, and paintings to be displayed at her memorial. New Orleans jazz recordings were peppered throughout the service, and at the end she led the crowd outside as Louis Armstrong sang "What a Wonderful World."

In planning ahead, Didi gave her loved ones a huge gift. She gave them the recipe for her funeral so all they had to do was put the ingredients together. Since it was Didi's "dish," they never had to question if they were making the right choices. This gave them the luxury of time to mourn, reunite, tell tales, and grieve with family and friends—just what Didi wanted.

We are not being facetious when we say we look forward to death. It's the road to it that can be a bit bumpy. We believe in a great afterlife; in fact, we feel life is the challenge and death is the reward.

EAT WELL; STAY FIT; DIE ANYWAY!

— *Anonymous*

CHAPTER 1

A FUNERAL PLANNER

THE WHY, THE HOW, THE PAYOFF

❊ ❊ ❊ ❊

Use it before you lose it!

(OR HOW TO USE THIS BOOK)

If *Grave Expectations* has come into your possession, either because you bought it or someone gave it to you—hang on to your hat! It will defy your preconceptions about what a funeral planner is. For example, if you don't laugh while reading this book, then we haven't done our job. Of course, just like life, there's more than laughing to this book. It includes guidance on everything from what to do with your body to DNR's to how to throw a blow-out party for the funeral. *Grave Expectations* gives you permission to memorialize your life on your own terms and in your own way. Ideally, once you've used the book, your dear friends and family members will have big grins on their faces at the end of your funeral and they'll say, "He (or she) would have loved this!"

---

countries with the highest average life expectancy (2007)

1. Andorra 83.52 years
2. Macau 82.27 years
3. Japan 82.02 years
4. San Marino 81.8 years
5. Singapore 81.8 years
6. Hong Kong 81.68 years
7. Gibraltar 80.9 years
8. Sweden 80.63 years
9. Switzerland 80.63 years
10. Australia 80.62 years

One can't advocate too much for planning a person's wrap party (aka funeral) before they die. Think about it: if someone is going down in an airplane, the likelihood that they'll have paper and pen to write a quick will with is virtually nil. Plus, they'll be thinking of other things like—"How do I pull that tab on the yellow thing? Who gets the oxygen first? Does it inflate or do I just breathe?" They'll be wishing they had watched the flight attendants more carefully.

Grave Expectations is a place where you can gather all those legal details that everyone knows they're supposed to address but a startling few of us actually get around to dealing with. For example, your living will, money, beneficiaries, funeral services, tax issues, and final wishes need to be taken care of. So when it's your time to go, your family and friends can grieve and not have to figure out where your safe deposit box is.

A Harris Interactive survey of the general population, done for Lawyers .com, found that 55 percent of Americans had no will. What if you never got around to divorcing your ex-wife and she got half of your estate, and the long-time girlfriend you never married and your four kids had to split the rest? Perhaps you converted to Judaism and your son, still a Catholic, wants to bury you in a Catholic ceremony? There can be a disconnect. Most people know they should tell someone about their wishes and address some of the legal requirements for end-of-life issues, but they keep putting it off. A few notes in this book (and drafting an actual will) can save so much agita!

We will take you by the hand and lead you through this inevitable journey that has a reputation for being difficult and morbid, and we don't believe it has to be either. In fact, we think you might have the time of your life—well—you may really enjoy it. When did you last spend time focusing on yourself without guilt? Doing this book will be a great gift to you and your family and

rank in world
for average
life expectancy
(2007)

....

36. United Kingdom 78.7 years
45. United States 78 years
103. China 72.88 years
142. Iraq 69.31 years
208. Afghanistan 43.77 years

friends. A potential payoff will be peace of mind and a reduction of guilt; that alone makes it worth the effort.

What do we mean when we say, "doing the book"? We're suggesting seeing what's most important to you and your loved ones, and then filling in the blanks provided throughout. Many people may want to start with the business section at the end; others may be more interested in what to do with the body. It doesn't really matter. Just dive in, browse, and go after the stuff that interests you most.

Another option might be to work with this book as inspiration strikes. You can pick it up and put it down like you might a journal. Travel with the book, take it to work, take it to family gatherings, do it in the bathroom. No place is too exalted or sacred to plan the end. (We recommend doing it with a couple of glasses of wine—it's good for your health and it reduces your inhibitions.) Remember, what you write is not set in stone. You can change the book as your life, thoughts, attitudes, and circumstances change.

Most of all, be free in your thinking—don't censor or limit yourself in planning as you go through the book. Two words of advice: *Don't worry!* This is not the time to be afraid. Don't be embarrassed or judgmental about any strange ideas you may have. Be aware that uncomfortable feelings and thoughts and reactions will come up—just let them rise to the surface and write them down

how we would use this book

Carmen would prefer to start with Chapter 2: "Who Am I or Who Was I?," which gives you the opportunity to write down your story and feelings about life. Carmen has no children to be her oral historians and has had some big times in life and doesn't want anyone to forget them. After that, she would do Chapter 9: "The Party"—because she loves to entertain and she wants people to have a good time!

Sue would prefer starting with Chapter 6: "Cremation, Ash Dispersal and Other Options"—because she wants to make sure no one sees her dead body in bizarre makeup and a bad hairdo. Then she would do the business section—or at least part of it, because she wants to be certain her body is used for science—as opposed to how she used it throughout her life!

anyway. You can always change your mind later. Be totally creative, put things in the book that inspire you, even if they feel inappropriate. Who is judging?

Grave Expectations gives you multiple opportunities to open up and talk about your fears and funeral—with your husband, wife, children, or parents. Just think about when you're writing away in this book and your spouse or kids walk by and ask you what you're doing and you get to say, "I'm planning my own funeral! Want to help me? Or, we can plan yours!" Doing the book with the ones you love can be an event in itself. Many people deny the fact of death, but by ignoring the inevitable (it's 100 percent fatal!), they miss the opportunity to commemorate and rejoice in their lives.

We believe everyone should express what they want at the end of their lives. To state the obvious, you will most likely end up planning your parents' funerals or your spouse's—but if you don't do it in advance, you will be doing it when you are grief-stricken, emotionally exhausted, and dreading having to deal with all the details. The popular wisdom is that after a loved one's death, it can be a relief to be distracted by planning the funeral and memorial service, but it's time better spent visiting your family and friends in peace and harmony and not stressing out about making the wrong decisions. You only need one neurotic family member to ruin a funeral!

Coping with a death can be one of the most vulnerable times in a person's life, and there's a danger of getting into disastrous, divisive family fights. It's a situation that lends itself to spending too much money on a funeral by not wanting to appear cheap or

leading causes of death in the united states

....

1. Heart disease
2. Cancer
3. Stroke

Lung cancer is number one and colon cancer is number two in leading causes of cancer deaths. Overall age-adjusted death rates for cancer rose between 1960 and 1990 and then reversed direction, declining by 10 percent between 1990 and 2002. Cancer death rates for males were 63 percent higher than for females in 1980 and 46 percent higher in 2002.

disrespectful. Without a plan, bereft families can be victimized by unscrupulous people in the death-care industry.

Ideally when you get done with this book, it should be a big mess! We have a vision of copies of *Grave Expectations* covered in post-it notes, dog-eared, written in, scratched out and changed, wine- and tear-stained pages, sections ripped out, big colorful hearts and doodles scrawled all over, and entire parts blacked out like when you get documents from the government through the Freedom of Information Act.

This book gives you a rare opportunity for initiating conversations about what to do when you or someone you know dies. We believe a person should prepare for any potentially dangerous, possibly fatal situations. Getting on a plane? Someone has cancer? Your town filled with crystal meth users? Great! See them for the opportunities they present. People are used to tiptoeing around death. But we say dive in! Look death in the eye and find the beauty there. Death is the one thing we have in common with every person on earth. So if you're shy, saying "Have you thought about your death?" to someone can be a great icebreaker. Many people are afraid of death because they believe it's the end of the line. You have to trust us here, death is something to look forward to; it's a gift—in particular, a graduation gift for all the struggles you've experienced in this life. So give yourself a reward for all you have accomplished and read on!

The $25 billion death-care industry handles 2.4 million people who die in the United States each year. Compare that to the movie industry, which took in $9.62 billion in a record year in 2007, and the porn industry, which took in $13.3 billion in 2006. Sex, entertainment, and death—life's essentials!

❋ ❋ ❋ ❋

CHAPTER 2

WHO AM I?
❋ OR ❋
WHO WAS I?

SOMETHING APPROACHING
THE SUM OF ME...

❋ ❋ ❋ ❋

his chapter is filled with questions about your likes and dislikes, your family history, your best memories, and the defining experiences in your life. This is like the first cocktail or two that loosens up the conversation.

Hopefully your answers to the questions in this section will be used at your service and/or party. It's essential that you feel free to skip over any part or question. Just answer the ones that resonate with you. Stream of consciousness works well. Don't get bogged down in trying to compose perfect images, thoughts, or sentences. Remember, this is meant to be a pleasure, not a chore—you're creating something positive and helpful for yourself and your family.

You'll find questions and comments in this chapter that may inspire terrific conversations, quiet contemplation, and surprising discoveries. If you do it right, you'll have the key elements for a eulogy and for the way you want to be remembered after you're gone.

heads up!

Every state has its own laws about funerals, burials, visitations, and other end-of-life issues covered in this book. We recommend that you check into what those restrictions are. You can start with your local funeral home or your official state website. Sadly, the law does not protect the deceased's wishes about anything to do with last rites, rituals, or receptions, so we recommend that you be really nice to whomever you choose to carry out your wishes. Or perhaps you might want to threaten—or rather encourage—them to carry out your requests in the will. We suggest a novel approach to getting what you want—we call it the "no play, no pay" clause!

HERE ARE SOME USEFUL TIPS ON HOW YOU SHOULD WORK THIS CHAPTER:

✣ Think of the following questions as diving boards into your memories. You might find that as you dive into the deep end you will recall experiences that you haven't thought of in years, so be prepared to encounter some intense emotions.

✣ Everyone's life is a great story—so write yours down here. This will help you appreciate it more. You might not feel your life has been successful or fulfilling, but we believe all lives are worthwhile.

✣ Answering these questions is like taking an inventory of yourself—it should be done periodically so you know what you've got and what you still need.

✣ This process of answering questions plants seeds in your mind that can grow at any time of your life. Just because the soil is old doesn't mean things can't sprout in it—it can be richer than young, fresh soil. Think of all that manure!

✣ Answering these questions is like looking back upon your life from a wiser perspective—you can give yourself a break. Like the saying goes: "You don't get to be old bein' no fool."

Your answers will let you relive the fun you've experienced and appreciate what you've been through as the process helps you weave a tapestry of your life—something that should be admired for its beauty.
Need we remind you to HAVE FUN?

Whether your choose to answer the questions in this section on your own or with others, they can truly inspire great moments and provoke all kinds of feelings, life changes, healings, reunions, and opportunities to be honest where it might have been difficult to do so otherwise. This will be an adventure! People may learn things about you they never realized before, even if you've known them your whole life. Your family and friends may have revelations of their own during this process. Here we go:

MEMORIES

MY FIRST MEMORY:

_____
_____

MY BEST MEMORY:

_____
_____

SOMETHING SCARY/FRIGHTENING THAT HAPPENED TO ME:

_____
_____

A MIRACLE THAT HAPPENED TO ME:

_____
_____

HAPPIEST TIMES OF MY LIFE:

_____
_____

HAPPIEST DAY OF MY LIFE:

_____
_____

THE CRAZIEST TIME OF MY LIFE:

_____

_____

MY MOST EXCITING EXPERIENCE:

_____

_____

MY FIRST LOVE WAS:

_____

_____

WHAT'S THAT SILLY STORY ABOUT ME THAT SOMEONE
REMEMBERS TO BRING UP AT EVERY HOLIDAY?

_____

_____

WHAT ABOUT THE STORIES THAT MAKE ME CRINGE?

_____

_____

FAMILY

FAMILY LEGENDS AND FAVORITE STORIES ABOUT ME:

_____

_____

FAMILY MOTTOS/FAVORITE EXPRESSIONS:

_____

_____

MOTHER'S MOTTOS/FAVORITE EXPRESSIONS:

_____

_____

FATHER'S MOTTOS/FAVORITE EXPRESSIONS:

_____

_____

THE BEST THING ABOUT MY CHILDHOOD WAS:

_____

_____

MY NICKNAMES:

_____

_____

FAVORITES

MY FAVORITE SAYINGS OR EXPRESSIONS ARE (DON'T CENSOR THEM):

_____

_____

MY FAVORITE PETS:

_____

_____

MY FAVORITE FAIRY TALE:

_____

_____

MY FAVORITE JOKE:

_____

_____

MY FAVORITE SONG/SONGS:

_____

_____

MY FAVORITE MUSICIANS:

_____

_____

MY FAVORITE KIND OF MUSIC:

_____

_____

MY FAVORITE MOVIE/MOVIES:

_____

_____

MY FAVORITE STARS (THE HUMAN KIND):

_____

_____

MY FAVORITE STARS (THE ASTRONOMICAL KIND):

_____

_____

MY FAVORITE CITY/CITIES:

_____

_____

MY FAVORITE COUNTRY/COUNTRIES:

_____

_____

MY FAVORITE VACATION:

_____

_____

MY FAVORITE ACTIVITIES:

_____

_____

MY FAVORITE SPORTS:

_____

_____

MY FAVORITE PLAYER:

_____

_____

MY FAVORITE TEAM:

_____

_____

MY FAVORITE FOODS:

_____

_____

WHAT I AM...
WHEN I WAS

MY GREATEST TALENT(S):

_____

_____

WHAT PEOPLE DON'T KNOW ABOUT ME:

_____

_____

WHEN I WAS REALLY YOUNG:

_____

_____

WHEN I WAS TEN I WAS:

_____

_____

WHEN I WAS TWENTY I WAS:

_____

_____

WHEN I WAS THIRTY I WAS:

_____

_____

WHEN I WAS FORTY I WAS:

_____

_____

WHEN I WAS FIFTY I WAS:

_____

_____

WHEN I WAS SIXTY I WAS:

_____

_____

WHEN I WAS SEVENTY I WAS:

_____

_____

WHEN I WAS EIGHTY I WAS:

_____

_____

WHEN I WAS OLDER THAN EIGHTY I WAS:

_____

_____

THE ACTOR WHO WOULD PLAY ME AT MY PRIME IN THE STORY OF MY LIFE:

_____

_____

THE ACTOR WHO WOULD PLAY ME AS I AM TODAY:

_____

_____

INTENTIONS

WHAT I HOPED TO ACCOMPLISH IN MY LIFE:

_____

_____

WHAT I STILL HOPE TO ACCOMPLISH IN MY LIFE:

_____

_____

WHAT I HOPED TO ACCOMPLISH IN MY LIFE BUT DIDN'T (AND WHY I DIDN'T):

_____

_____

WHAT I ACTUALLY ACCOMPLISHED WITH MY LIFE:

_____

_____

WHICH WAS MORE IMPORTANT TO ME—
MY JOB, MY PERSONAL LIFE, OR MY SPIRITUAL LIFE? WHY?

_____

_____

AT THE END I WAS/AM/WANT TO BE:

_____

_____

WHAT IS THE ONE ADJECTIVE I'D MOST LIKE TO BE REMEMBERED BY?

_____

_____

ANY REGRETS? (COME ON, DON'T LIE):

_____

_____

DID I FOOL ANYONE IN A MAJOR WAY?
IF SO, HOW AND WHY AND WHAT DID I DO?

_____

_____

I DON'T KNOW WHY I EVER:

_____

_____

IF I CAN SEND SOMEONE A SIGN FROM THE OTHER SIDE, I'LL TRY TO:

_____

_____

DISLIKES

A FOOD I HATE OR JUST DISLIKE:

_____

_____

SOMEONE WHO MADE MY LIFE MISERABLE:

_____

_____

AN ERA OF FASHION THAT I HATED:

_____

_____

THE KIND OF MUSIC I HATE OR JUST DISLIKE:

_____

_____

AN ACTIVITY THAT I HATE:

_____

_____

AN EXPRESSION THAT JUST MAKES MY SKIN CRAWL:

_____

_____

THE BIGGEST LIE I'VE EVER HEARD:

_____

_____

THE WORST PRESIDENT IN THE HISTORY OF THE UNITED STATES:

_____

_____

SPIRIT

WHEN DID FATE ENTER MY LIFE AND CHANGE IT DRAMATICALLY?

_____

_____

SOMETHING I OVERCAME AGAINST ALL ODDS WAS:

_____

_____

I'M PROUD OF:

_____

_____

I'M NOT PROUD OF:

_____

_____

MY BIGGEST MISTAKE WAS:

_____

_____

I'VE HAD A LONG AFFAIR WITH
(A PERSON, FOOD, SPORTS TEAM, SHOW, WHATEVER):

_____

_____

PEOPLE WHO INSPIRE/INSPIRED ME:

_____

_____

MY SPIRITUAL TEACHER/TEACHERS:

_____

_____

LIFE-CHANGING BOOKS:

_____

_____

WHAT I LIKE MOST ABOUT MYSELF:

_____

_____

WHAT I DISLIKE MOST ABOUT MYSELF:

_____

_____

IN GENERAL, AM I HAPPY WITH MY LIFE? WHY?

_____

_____

I AM THANKFUL FOR:

_____

_____

SOME OF THE MOST IMPORTANT RELATIONSHIPS IN MY LIFE:

_____

_____

WHAT MAKES THOSE RELATIONSHIPS SO SPECIAL?

_____

_____

DO I BELIEVE IN A WORLD BEYOND THIS ONE?
IF SO, WHAT DO I THINK IT'S LIKE?

_____

_____

WHAT, IF ANY, CONTACT HAVE I HAD WITH THE OTHER SIDE?

_____

_____

FOR ME, GOD IS:

_____

_____

FOR ME, THE UNIVERSE IS:

_____

_____

HOW DO I FEEL ABOUT DYING?

_____

_____

I BELIEVE THAT AFTER I DIE I WILL:

_____

_____

So, do you feel better? We wish we had been able to have this experience—to "do" this chapter—with our own parents before they died. We believe that we would have learned things about them that could have been revelatory—making us understand them in new and deeper ways and perhaps significantly changing our relationships with them, and in the process perhaps learning more about ourselves.

CHAPTER 3

THE VISITATION/ VIEWING

WAKE UP TO THE POSSIBILITIES!

Now that your head is full of memories, stories, and what-ifs from the work you did in the last chapter, we're going to tell you how your family and friends can enjoy a final "visit" with you after you're gone.

Also known as the viewing or the wake, the visitation is a bit like your debut as a dead person. This is the time before the actual funeral service for those who need to come to terms with your death. There are a lot of options to choose from, and we encourage you to discuss this with your loved ones in advance. It will be a very tender time for your family and friends. Unlike many of the other parts of this book, the visitation is more about your family and friends than it is about you. Yes, you'll be the center of attention, but this is an event they must participate in, since being around your dead body (or not) comes with some special considerations.

When someone died in Victorian America, windows were draped in black, black wreaths decorated the doorways, and black crepe hanging outside the home all served notice to neighbors that a death had occured. All mirrors in the house were covered, and if one of them broke, it was believed that someone else in the home would soon die. If there was a clock in the room of the deceased, it had to be stopped at the death hour, or the family would have bad luck. Finally, the body had to be carried out of the house feet first so it couldn't look back and entice others to follow it into death.

You might want to make an agreement with your family that when the time comes, they have your permission to do what they feel is best, in the event they disagree with your wishes. (After all, you won't be there and your negotiating skills will be diminished.) Try to be as flexible as possible, yet indicate where you are absolutely not willing to compromise.

Every state has its own laws about funerals, burials, visitations, and other end-of-life issues. We recommend you check into what those restrictions are. You can start with your local funeral home or your official state website.

Remember—the law does not protect the deceased's wishes about anything to do with last rites, rituals, or receptions, so we recommend that you be really nice to whomever you choose to carry out your wishes. Or perhaps you might want to threaten—or rather encourage—them to carry out your wishes in your will. We suggest a novel approach to getting what you want—we call it the "No Play, No Pay" clause.

Undertaking basically came from three different professions. Cabinetmakers frequently became undertakers, as they built the coffins. Liverymen became undertakers, as they transported the coffins, and in times of epidemics these dangerous services were especially needed. Midwives performed considerable undertaking duties, since approximately 35 percent of childbirths in the eighteenth and nineteenth centuries resulted in death of the baby, as well as many of the mothers.

Keep in mind that the purpose of the visitation/viewing is to provide support and ease the survivors through your transition from life to death. It's a time to tell stories, give prayers, condolences, and support, and share in the grief. And yet, like the service and party, the viewing may be as quiet or as extravagant as you wish. Like any good party planner, think about the mood you want to create—for example, somber, festive, funny (try a big poster that says LAUGH over the door when you walk in), dirgelike (do you want people to sob uncontrollably?), reverent or irreverent, etc. Of course the visitation or viewing is very dependent on people's religious beliefs—or lack of them.

Talk about a viewing with a variety of moods! In 1599, in Palermo, Italy, Capuchin monks discovered a mysterious preservative in their catacombs. Because of that, over 8,000 people chose to be "buried" there. Visitors now wander among the mummies, most of them hanging in long rows on the walls. They're divided by profession, age, class, sex, and even by their virginity. Velasquez, the famous painter, rests there. The oldest displayed corpses are from the sixteenth century—the youngest is from 1920—two-year-old Rosalia Lombaro, who was embalmed, is perfectly preserved and is called "Sleeping Beauty." Each corpse has an individual expression—some laugh maniacally, some are dreamy, some look as if they just got slapped.

TIME TO JOT DOWN SOME OF YOUR THOUGHTS
AND IDEAS CONCERNING YOUR VISITATION:

DO YOU WANT TO HAVE A VIEWING/VISITATION?

_____

_____

IF SO, DO YOU MIND PEOPLE SEEING YOUR BODY?
IN OTHER WORDS: OPEN OR CLOSED CASKET?

_____

_____

IF YOU ARE COMFORTABLE ABOUT DISPLAYING YOUR BODY, WHERE
WOULD YOU LIKE TO BE VIEWED? FUNERAL HOME, FAMILY HOME,
RELIGIOUS CENTER, OR SOMEWHERE ELSE?

_____

_____

IF YOU DON'T WANT A "PUBLIC" VIEWING, DO YOU WANT PEOPLE TO
COME TO YOUR HOME OR VISIT A FRIEND OR FAMILY MEMBER'S HOME
TO PAY THEIR RESPECTS?

_____

_____

Saints are on display for hundreds of years, while Lenin's body has only been on view over 80 years. Upkeep includes a pump inside his body to control humidity, frequent rejuvenation with biochemical baths (no dry skin here!), cameras and equipment to monitor the skin color, and a new set of clothes every 3 years. Some scientists say Lenin's body will never decay.

Of course, if you're famous and a public figure of some sort—for example, John F. Kennedy, Martin Luther King, Jr., Abraham Lincoln, Ayatollah Khomeini, Pope John Paul II, Evita Peron, Franklin Delano Roosevelt, Ronald Reagan, Rosa Parks—your body is no longer your own. You may be put on display for days like some kind of rare orchid or a meteorite from outer space. People may line up to catch a glimpse of you—or even to touch your body. Why? We have our theories, mostly having to do with clichés like closure and recognition that life has truly ended. It's kind of a compliment when you think of it. However, if you aren't famous enough for a state viewing and funeral, then probably something more modest is in order.

IF YOU WANT TO HAVE A VIEWING, WHAT DO YOU WANT TO WEAR?

_____

_____

Many people want to, or feel they have to, wear their dress-up clothes when they're on display—for instance, that suit you bought for all those funerals you had to attend. (Don't you love the irony?) Well, we recommend you consider wearing something that is representative of your daily life. Wear your favorite Hawaiian shirt; an outfit you've been saving for your daughter's wedding (the one who never got married); your favorite sports team's uniform or regalia; your secret crown; professional attire like a judge's robe, nurse's uniform, or circus costume; if you were a closet cross dresser, now's the time to come out; clerical robes; chef's hat; rodeo outfit; church lady attire (don't forget the large hat and the white gloves); golf clothes with your favorite golf club; that tie that you love but everyone else hates; your "Do these pants make me look fat?" pants. You get the idea. Just don't let anyone shame you into wearing something other than what you truly desire.

DO YOU WANT TO WEAR JEWELRY? IF SO, WHAT ITEMS?

_____

_____

What our parents wanted

Sue's mother did not want a visitation or a funeral, she just wanted to be burned and buried. Her children and a few friends attended—against her wishes—a modest graveside service. She planned the end of her life like she lived it—with great stubbornness and not giving a damn what others thought.

Carmen's father, however, wanted a visitation at his home for hundreds of people. He wanted to see their faces from the other side one last time. Instead of a funeral, he wanted a great big party several months later that everyone who knew and loved him would be able to attend. On the last night of his life, Carmen and her father stayed awake until dawn planning the festivities down to every detail, including the pictures and memorabilia to be displayed, which flowers from his garden to be placed around the house, the recipe for the cheese garlic grits, and who was designated to grill the venison sausage. Everyone had a great time! To this day Carmen has fond memories of an event that could have been predominantly sorrowful—a testament to preplanning.

You'll be dead, so the words gaudy, tasteless, ostentatious and too ethnic will mean nothing to you. Drape yourself in gold if that's what you've always wanted to do, or pare it down and be tasteful. Pieces with sentimental value are always good, even the ugly poodle pin your son gave you when he was five. Don't worry, it will all be removed and returned to whomever you've designated to receive it.

DO YOU HAVE ANY SPECIAL MAKEUP REQUESTS?
(THIS GOES FOR WOMEN AND MEN!)

It can still happen. Eighty-one-year-old Chilean Feliberto Carrasco stunned his grieving family and himself by waking up in a coffin at his own wake. Earlier, when his family discovered his cold and limp body, they failed to call a doctor and called a funeral home instead. He was dressed in his finest suit for the funeral. The only discomfort Feliberto expressed was that he was a bit thirsty.

For example, you may have worn one lipstick color for years and want only that color. (If Chanel hasn't discontinued it—this is one reason to always keep a spare tube of your favorite color on hand.) What nail color do you want? We recommend you insist that no outlandish makeup schemes be carried out by a creatively starved undertaker's assistant who missed his or her chance to work on Broadway; no blue eye shadow, no sparkly accents, and no Marilyn Monroe "beauty" spot, unless that's your look. We had one young Chinese American cashier at Barnes and Noble tell us that she hated the idea that her mother would use the traditional white-mask makeup at her funeral. The clerk had already written down the clothes, make up and nail polish that she herself wanted for her own funeral.

DO YOU WANT PHOTOS DISPLAYED AND/OR VIDEOS PLAYED? WHICH ONES?

_____

_____

If you say "yes," make sure they are flattering and are ones you have chosen. Some people's idea of attractive may be very different from your own, which is why we recommend you choose the photos. Do not use use high-resolution photographs—unless the photographer has carefully defocused the shot. Every wrinkle will have a life of its own. We are not kidding. Of course, if you want to *scare* people, go ahead. Like they won't be edgy already with your dead body there! The days of photography when heavy softening filters were routinely used are over. Think how Marlene Dietrich, Bette Davis, or Joan Crawford would have looked like without makeup and filters—pretty scary!

The photos that you choose may be put on one of the many photo-sharing websites, such as Flickr.com or the various memorial sites, for your family and friends to access images of you.

You may compile a short video for the service, if you wish. Collect all your favorite moments on DVD (your old tape and film can be transferred to a disk) and have someone under ten put it together. Why not have a two-part video, where you create your own section with specific music, structure, and events of your life? Then your family can add a section, to give their impressions of you. In some cases, this would be quite a contrast.

Today there are interesting things be-

In the 1800s Americans were not directly affected by the bereavement of Queen Victoria, but they were influenced by her mourning fashion and customs. During the initial phase of grieving, women went without jewelry but happily began to wear it during the second stage. Jewelry that contained hair was very popular; the fad came from Europe and caught on in the United States during the Civil War as soldiers left home to fight. After the death of her husband, Mary Todd Lincoln summoned a messenger to request a lock of the president's hair, which she made into a locket.

ing done with live broadcasts of visitations and funerals over the Internet. You can find these companies on the web or let your fingers do the walking through the Yellow Pages. And of course you can also discuss a web broadcast with your funeral director. This option, however, is not available everywhere.

> Ladies, don't let your boys become undertakers. They will be on-call 24/7, 365 days a year. No holiday or event (including your own funeral) is exempt!

DO YOU WANT MUSIC? IF SO, WHAT MUSIC?
DO YOU WANT IT TO BE LIVE OR RECORDED?

_____

_____

_____

We've already done the work of compiling a wild, comprehensive list of music choices—take a peek at chapter nine for those ideas. However, there are a couple of differences between the ideal music for a visitation and the ideal music for a funeral. First, we suggest you have your favorite visitation music on a loop, which means that it plays over and over. It should be easy to find someone with a computer who can do this for you. The music can be background music that creates the mood you want the event to have. It can conjure up memories of good times, difficult times, youthful times, or the golden years. Anyway, choose your favorite songs, bands, moods, nature sounds, etc., and make arrangements to have them played at your visitation. It's our opinion that having live

> Some viewings never end. The Catholic Church has said that the dozens of saints on view in various churches are "incorrupt"—that is, their bodies will not decay. Many are said to have a sweet smell. Saint Silvan apparently died in 350 A.D. and looks amazingly fresh, like he just fainted and fell back. The Church does not recognize any saint as incorruptible if they have been embalmed.

music here would be more of a distraction than adding anything to the tone you may want to create. With live music, the focus may be more on the performers than on coming to terms with the death of a loved one—in this case you. Keep the visitation focused on you; that's what people will want and need.

If you decide to have a live band or performer at the visitation, then we suggest you include specifics for your loved ones, including contact information.

BAND OR PERFORMER AND CONTACT INFORMATION:

_____

_____

WHAT FLOWERS, PLANTS OR MEMENTOS WOULD YOU PREFER?

_____

_____

_____

We love flowers of all kinds, and we love all sorts of arrangements. We just don't like those big "I've just won the Kentucky Derby" carnation horseshoe arrangements—unless, of course, you were a jockey and actually won the race!

Most of all, we recommend the gifts that keep on giving—like young trees, bulbs, flowering plants, and shrubs that can become living memorials for years or lifetimes to come. Think of a hydrangea bush that makes your family and friends remember you every season it blooms. This is your time to decide what kinds of flowers or plants that you prefer, and don't be shy about expressing it. Plants and flowers can

Among popular Victorian "memento mori"—objects that remind you that you will die—were photos of the dead. These were kept as mementos of loved ones, sometimes the only images of the departed that existed. Parents would pose with their dead children, propped up and with eyes open, to look as if they were still alive. They were also made to look as if they had just fallen asleep. Deceased adults were commonly photographed sitting in a chair. In some areas of the world, the practice still exists—especially for people who are considered holy.

In nineteenth-century America, the dead were laid out at home, and friends would bring flowers not only as a gift but also to mask the odor of the decaying body.

have powerful effects on people, so think of what your survivors would want to have to remember you over the years. When they see a plant or tree that was given in your memory, it's like having a little visit from you.

WHAT'S THE NAME AND CONTACT INFORMATION OF YOUR FAVORITE FLORIST OR NURSERY?

_____

_____

Here's a very important suggestion: One of the best things you can do for your family is to give them your personal and professional e-mail list or your address book. Can you imagine the nightmare of trying to locate someone's friends and business associates without leads? Try not to give that drama to your loved ones at such a painful time. In fact, why not send your e-mail list to someone right now, and/or get your address book copied and given to a person you trust. If you have some names that you don't want to be made public at this time, put them in a sealed envelope and keep it in this book.

There continues to be a taboo against uttering a deceased's name or any words that sound similar in certain cultures, including Siberia, Southern India, the Sahara, Japan, the Philippines, East Africa, Borneo, Madagascar, Tasmania, and Southern Australia, to name a few. Some go so far as to change their names if it is the same or similar to that of the deceased's.

MORE THOUGHTS ON THE VISITATION/VIEWING:

_____

_____

_____

_____

_____

_____

_____

_____

_____

_____

_____

_____

_____

_____

_____

_____

_____

_____

_____

_____

_____

_____

_____

_____

"Show me the manner in which a nation cares for its dead, and I will measure with mathematical exactness its respect for the laws of order and society."

—William Gladstone, Prime Minister of the United Kingdom, (1809–1898)

TRADITIONAL BURIAL

THE REMAINS OF YOU

What to do with your body is probably the most charged decision of all the choices you will make in planning your exit. Or not. We've seen families fight over what to do with the body because the deceased hadn't left instructions for anyone before they died. Perhaps you have no doubt in your mind about what you want done with your remains, but your family may have other ideas. It's best to bring it out into the open now and have those fights before you die. We rather enjoy a good fight now and then; it hones the debating skills.

What to do with your body may seem like an unpleasant topic, but we have found it can actually inspire a lively, fascinating, even bizarre discussion. The future is now, there is a sea change happening here, and you will be amazed at what scientists, entrepreneurs, and crackpots have come up with for body disposal. Choice is good, no? Have fun with the possibilities, as we have encouraged you to do with everything else.

Since the early nineteenth century, the City of New York has laid to rest the bodies of their indigent and forgotten men and women in potter's fields. Three popular green spaces in Manhattan—Madison Square Park, Washington Square Park, and Bryant Park—started out as potter's fields. Over the years, many souls were moved from one burial ground to another, until they found a final resting place on the island of Hart Field in Long Island Sound. There are about 600,000 dead buried there, with approximately 8,000 additional burials occurring per year.

TRADITIONAL BURIAL
old-fashioned but still a good choice

This section addresses the traditional burial, meaning you put the old vehicle in the garage and seal it up permanently! We understand that you may actually have an attachment to your body. No surprise there. We kind of like ours. We're not trying to push our philosophy on anyone, but just for purposes of full disclosure, we feel the soul leaves the body and it is no longer you—it is the remains of a wonderful gift from God that has ceased functioning. The phone's dead and a new battery just won't make it work again. So, we don't feel the need to preserve our bodies in any way.

If you choose to be buried, you are joining a tradition that has endured for thousands of years. It's cool to think the pyramids are just great big cemetery plots with lots of fancy stonework. And the ancient Egyptians were very wise, except when they killed servants, slaves, animals, even other family members and noblemen to keep the king company and to serve him beyond the grave. Sounds goofy now, but they actually did that. We know you're not that bad-mannered. You'll have lots of fun in heaven without killing the family and taking them along for the ride. No need to force the company to stay past the end of the party!

If you decide on your body being buried, it does not mean you need to be embalmed, but you should decide where you want to be put. This can be a delightful process if you live in parts of the country where you have lots of options or if you like to travel. Today, lots of states allow you to be buried almost anywhere—on your farm, in a state park (though just your ashes, and only with permission), next to the highway (a trucker's paradise!), in your neighbors' flower garden just to piss them off. But you do need to check your state's website for rules and regulations, and the same goes for your state or national park websites if you have that inclination. With some cemeteries, if you pay in advance, you can save thousands—so it's always good to look into that option. Just be aware that the cemetery may no longer be there when your time comes.

The choice does get complicated if you want to be buried in a family plot. Say you pay for it and then you get divorced. Or your parents have separate family plots—whose do you choose? Or perhaps you buy your plot and someone you hate buys the one next to it—it's kind of like being seated at a restaurant next to someone you can't stand and then you have to ask to be moved, which results in potentially negative ramifications from the wait staff. So, our motto is, "It's good to think ahead." But life is complicated so all this is par for the course. Speaking of par for the course, you can't be buried on a golf course, but some people have had their ashes scattered on their favorite hole—kind of gives you a new outlook on getting stuck in a sand trap. (Okay, maybe you can end up on a golf course. Donald Trump has filed paperwork to build a wedding chapel on his 525-acre golf course in Bedminster, New Jersey. He told the Star-Ledger of Newark that he intends to later convert the building into a mausoleum for his family and himself.)

Burial at sea can be an attractive alternative to being buried in the ground. There are many services all over the country that are willing to take you on one last cruise—no return trip ticket necessary. If you like the idea of sleeping with the fishes (hopefully there won't be any sharks in the area), this service may be for you. Traditionally sea burial has been primarily for navy veterans, but it can be quite moving and appropriate for those who love the ocean.

Veterans with honorable discharges are entitled to be buried in military cemeteries around the country. Two things we can say are that the cemeteries are all really beautiful, nicely maintained, and peaceful. Plus, a wife can be buried on top of her husband. (If he dies first, of course. This may seem like a joke, but it's not.) Check out the United States Department of Veterans Affairs website at www.cem.va.gov/. It's full of great information. Go to the FAQ section and type in "Burial." Every bit of information you need and didn't even know you needed comes right up. Did you know that a civilian spouse may be buried in a veteran's

Large crowds at Chinese funerals are viewed as a mark of honor for the deceased. And what better way to draw a crowd than hiring strippers to perform at the service? Unfortunately for some crowd pleasers, the Chinese government made the bump-and-grind custom illegal in 2006. They now have a hotline where disturbed citizens can report "funeral misdeeds" and receive cash rewards. The Taiwanese, on the other hand, invite strippers to perform while friends and family give hard-core commentary on the deceased's virility.

graveyard even if he or she predeceases the military spouse? They even take the kids under some circumstances.

As mentioned earlier, you don't have to be embalmed to be buried in a conventional cemetery—only if, after dying, you're traveling across certain state lines (check with your state government) and/or if you want to have a public viewing. You may have a private family viewing without being embalmed. If you choose to be embalmed, we thought you should know a bit about what you're getting into—or rather, what exactly is getting into you. That would be embalming fluid, composed of formaldehyde, methanol, ethanol, and other solvents. Trust us, you don't want to hang around these chemicals for long; they're extremely carcinogenic. Anyway, all the fluids in the body are forced out and replaced by the embalming fluid. These techniques have essentially not changed since the Civil War. Look up Vladimir Lenin on the Internet—his embalmed body is still in great shape and a popular tourist attraction in Russia. What a country—we have Disneyland and they visit dead guys' bodies on display!

If you've decided to be buried, circle your answers to the following questions to guide your family and friends as to what your wishes are:

DO YOU WANT A TRADITIONAL BURIAL?

YES / NO

DO YOU WANT TO BE EMBALMED?

YES / NO

HOW WOULD YOU LIKE ME TO WRAP THAT?

Nowadays it seems like you can buy coffins with every design, color, or theme possible. It's a "Trick My Coffin" world. They can be covered in stars, flowers, motorcycles, your favorite song, Da Vinci's "Last Supper," your country's flag, movie stars' portraits, Star Wars characters, poems, messages, sports teams' insignias, angels, religious figures, photos of any sort, and custom designs—you name it, the sky's the limit. Coffins can be made in the shape of a big tropical fish, a spaceship, a Louis Vuitton duffle bag, a Rolls Royce, a corkscrew, a pink ballet slipper, and the cockpit of a WWII Spitfire fighter plane. Just go online and you can find an amazing selection. Of course, we also like the idea of a plain pine box. Minimalism can be very classy.

Most of the really decorative coffins these days are made from cardboard, but there is a vast selection of materials to choose from, including basketwork, fiberglass, and all kinds of wood, bamboo, crystal, and stone. If you like choosing tile for your bathroom, you'll love choosing your custom coffin!

Funeral directors can help in making choices about your funeral arrangements, as they have the resources and the experience. Most people aren't present to have their own coffin discussion, however, since they waited too long. That's why we recommend interviewing funeral directors and going into the minutia of funeral practices and pricing before it's too late. There is an unbelievable range of coffin costs in addition to designs. Spending more money

It was once the custom in Ireland to remove the nails from coffins immediately before lowering them into the grave, in the belief that the dead would then have no difficulty in freeing themselves on the day of Resurrection.

doesn't mean you're going to get a better casket. This is where you can blow lots of money or be more frugal and possibly save the cash for a big party.

We are bargain shoppers and like to get the most for our money, so we don't prefer those massive, tanklike metal caskets that look like you can storm the beaches of Okinawa or survive a nuclear attack. We think buying one of those expensive caskets is like buying a car and using it only once or like buying a really expensive wedding dress and wearing it only one time. At least the wedding dress has a chance of playing a second act—for example on eBay or for your daughter—but not the casket.

For the most part, funeral directors are a caring, sensitive bunch, but beware because not all funeral directors play by the rules. Between 2003 and 2006 the nonprofit Funeral Consumers Alliance Inc. found that in a study of 272 funeral homes from six states, 86.7 percent had at least one Federal Trade Commission (FTC) rule violation and most had many more. For this reason, ask questions, be skeptical, and especially trust that little voice of doubt whenever it whispers in your ear.

The Federal Trade Commission passed the Funeral Act in 1984. For the first time, funeral homes had to provide itemized price lists to the deceased's family. They were banned from embalming bodies without explicit permission, and they were required to make all options for embalming, cremation, and burial very clear. As a result, between 1960 and 1993, the percentage of per capita income spent on funerals fell by half.

This next piece of advice is for those who don't have or don't want to spend thousands on a casket for a traditional burial: do not be intimidated by any funeral director into spending too much and/or more than you can afford on a casket! We feel really strongly about this and want to give you a little pep talk on standing up to funeral home bullies trying to squeeze a bunch of money out of you, especially when you are in an extremely vulnerable position.

A few states such as Alabama, Georgia, Louisiana, Oklahoma, South Carolina, and Virginia do not permit anyone other than a mortician to sell a casket or a coffin, so forget the beautiful, custom-tailored cardboard coffins or the discount caskets from Costco (no kidding). If you or your family is ever in the position of looking for a reasonably priced coffin, do not be shamed into overspending. As one reporter for the *Chicago Sun-Times* found out when her funeral shopper companion asked a funeral director if there wasn't something less expensive than the $2,000+ casket on display: "They led us to a hall on the way to the boiler room." Another woman was taken to a basement that was filled with cobwebs. Another shopper was subjected to the icy sneer: "Oh . . . you want the welfare casket?" Don't let anyone push you around or embarrass you. Go to the Internet right now and check out all the options you have to choose from. No matter what they say, stay strong in your conviction to save your family this decision and to carry out your mission, especially if you want to be frugal and not blow your family fortune on temporary housing in a miniature condo-coffin.

Japanese funerals are among the most expensive in the world—the average price is around $40,000. Some of the high costs are due to lack of available funeral plots, and relatives—afraid of seeming cheap—are reluctant to negotiate prices. The system involves lots of bribes and price-fixing between the funeral homes, florists, priests, and even the hospitals that send the bodies their way.

That said, if the spirit moves you, we also totally support blowing a fortune on buying the Rolls Royce of coffins—a $20,000 bronze/gold number with the additional $10,000 bronze "security box"—no messy drips or embarrassing odors!—also known as the "burial vault." (Some states require burial vaults, so

Hallstatt, Austria, is a tiny town situated between a lake and a mountain. Land for burial is very scarce. The town's solution to this problem since the early 1700s has been to bury the dead in coffins for about twelve years, dig them up, clean off the bones, and then put them on exhibit in the chapel. There are over 600 skulls on display, many of them painted with the names of the deceased, their professions, and dates of death. The bones are neatly placed on shelves below the skulls. Since the 1960s, cremation has been used to solve the space problem.

In 1963, Jessica Mitford published *The American Way of Death*, in which she pointed out that in 1960, Americans spent more on funerals than on higher education.

check your state laws.) But why stop there? Get a casket/coffin in the shape of a Nike shoe, cell phone, lion, wingtip, machine gun, or spring onion. In our search for so-called "fantasy coffins," the most creative ones come out of Ghana. Who knew?

Here are some key questions to answer when considering what type of coffin is best for you:

WHAT KIND OF COFFIN DO YOU WANT?

_____

_____

HOW MUCH DO YOU WANT TO SPEND ON A COFFIN?

_____

_____

DO YOU WANT TO BUY THE COFFIN IN ADVANCE (THE "LAYAWAY" PLAN)?

_____

_____

IF YOU AREN'T REQUIRED BY LAW TO HAVE ONE OF THOSE BURIAL VAULTS OR GRAVE LINERS, DO YOU WANT ONE ANYWAY? WHAT KIND?

_____

_____

BUYER BEWARE: If you want to buy the coffin in advance, many coffin companies go out of business and might not be there when you're ready. (That's a euphemism for when you die.) So you may want to take it home with you or store it somewhere. In our opinion, this is not a great option for you or your loved ones. ("Hey Mom, why don't we store the Christmas ornaments in your coffin?")

MARKING YOUR TURF

When it comes to headstones or markers, you can be as creative and unique as you want to be. We think it's good to stand out in a crowd and distinguish yourself from the other slabs. We like the headstones that are attached to a bench. Think about it—where are your mourners going to sit? Right on top of you? Or are they just going to stand there until they get too tired? Be a good host!

One of the best headstones we've seen to date is the "The Bronze Dove" created by a company called Rock of Ages. It's a beautiful dove executed in bronze that sits atop a granite boulder. The position of the wings makes it look as if the bird has just landed. The more we study various monuments, the more we like the weeping angel. We're also big fans of the stud-angel memorial of St. Michael. He's got six-pack abs—we're not kidding! We also like headstones that look like a book.

If you want a headstone or grave marker, what do you want on it? Nowadays you have the option, in certain cemeteries, to put a disk with recorded information embedded in your headstone. There is also a solar-powered tombstone now available for that multimedia effect—pictures, music, etc.—all on a seven-inch screen.

Continue the creative thinking here that we recommend throughout the book. Do you want to leave a last message to the world? (Keep it clean!) Most likely your family will want to add something as well. Do you have a favorite saying? Is there a piece of advice you'd like to give, a favorite passage, a favorite line from a song? (for

Sarah Bernhardt, one the most famous actresses of all time, kept a coffin at home, which was said to be lined with letters from her numerous lovers. She kept the coffin in her boudoir and occasionally slept in it. She even allowed herself to be photographed there.

example, Peggy Lee's "Is That All There Is?"), or maybe a certain sentiment—consider humorous ones as well as serious ones—like:

❖ "And for this I left your mother?"
❖ "Free at last, free at last. Thank God Almighty, I'm free at last!" (Martin Luther King Jr.)
❖ "Come On Down, Charlie Bailey!"
❖ "Go to Heaven for the climate, Hell for the company." (Mark Twain)
❖ "Blow Me!" (Think of the impact this would have on someone just strolling through the graveyard reading headstones.)
❖ "I had no idea when I chose Door Number 3 . . . "
❖ "So Long, Suckers!"
❖ "Because I could not stop for Death, He kindly stopped for me." (Emily Dickinson)
❖ "Hey! I broke on through to the Other Side!"
❖ "Yankees Rule!"
❖ "You're searching, Joe, for things that don't exist; I mean beginnings. Ends and beginnings—there are no such things. There are only middles." (Robert Frost)
❖ "Come on in—the dirt's fine!"
❖ "Where's the meat? I am the meat!"
❖ "In heaven all the interesting people are missing." (Friedrich Nietzsche)
❖ "Come out of the circle of time, and into the circle of love." (Rumi)

Alexander the Great loved his pet dog Peritas so much that, after her death, he led a formal funeral procession to her grave and erected a large stone monument on the site. She had given her life to save his life during an assault by the troops of Persia's Darius III, when she leapt and bit the lip of an elephant charging her master. In her honor, Alexander named a city after her that still exists today.

Do you like the whacky variety? We think since there are a variety of people in the world, there should be a variety of headstone sayings—don't just stick to the serious ones or the expected quotes. We hate to repeat ourselves, but the Internet is wonderful for getting great quotes about

> Laura Huxley gave her husband Aldous Huxley on his deathbed, at his request, two injections of 100 mg of LSD.

specific subjects. It's amazing, really. In addition to using *death* as a search word, try different things like *freedom, heaven, the end, time, beginnings, graduation, joy, baseball,* etc. Or just put in a famous person's name, someone you admire—a musician, a holy man, a poet, a comedian, novelist, civil rights leader, football coach—you get the idea.

The point is that you should say something that reflects something about you—words that, fifty or a hundred years from now when strangers walk by your headstone, will stop them and make them reflect on who you were and what your life was like. This is actually a return to an earlier tradition where people wanted to leave a permanent record of who they were. Have you walked through old graveyards reading the headstones? You frequently get a real feeling for the people and what they went through. Of course, stone engraving has always been expensive, so it may be necessary to use an economy of words. Today we do have the technology to incorporate permanent digital recordings of the deceased, giving full pictures of their lives. Just think if we had recordings of the lives of those people in the very old graveyards—it would be fascinating!

DO YOU WANT A HEADSTONE OR A GRAVE MARKER?

WHAT DO YOU WANT IT TO SAY?

_____

_____

A crypt is a fortified space constructed of reinforced concrete, steel, and waterproof materials—sort of like a bunker for the dead. It holds casketed remains with room for up to several family members. (Don't blame us if you argue in the afterlife!) It can hold coffins as well as urns of cremated remains.

DO YOU WANT INTERMENT IN A CRYPT? IF SO, WHAT KIND?

_____

_____

Sati or *suttee*, which means "virtuous woman," is the former Hindu practice of a widow burning herself on her husband's funeral pyre. Going sati in India was not obligatory, but many women preferred being burned alive to living the cursed life of a widow. Others believed it was an honor and that once they died, they would be worshipped like a goddess.

It's never too late to buy a fortress! Continuing with the bunker mentality, a mausoleum is an aboveground crypt. While most of us think that a mausoleum is for wealthy people, the price is comparable to the cost of interment in a plot with an upright monument. A big advantage of a mausoleum is that they are clean and dry and can hold other people that you've chosen, or who have chosen you.

If you've got the money, why not feed your ego and go for a Greek temple or a church? If you really want to get inspired, go look at ancient history books or stroll through large cemeteries and get some design ideas.

DO YOU WANT A MAUSOLEUM? IF SO, WHAT KIND?

_____

_____

IF YOU CHOOSE A CRYPT OR MAUSOLEUM, WHO, IF ANYONE,
DO YOU WANT TO BE IN THERE WITH YOU?

_____

_____

HE AIN'T HEAVY, HE'S MY BROTHER (MOTHER, SISTER, WHATEVER...)

If you've decided to opt for a traditional burial, you're going to need some pall-bearers. Choose six to eight people, preferably ones who can carry a heavy load—several hundred pounds of metal, velvet, various stuffings, and dead weight (meaning you). Depending on how much you weigh, your group of pall-bearers could be packin' 300 to 400 pounds easily! Or rather, not so easily. That means they should be young and vital (unless they're old and buff). Perhaps you can cruise your local gyms for some candidates. Why not try dating them first? It's good to know your pallbearers well.

We do recommend asking people in advance if they would agree to be a pallbearer. Some people are physically capable but not emotionally prepared for the challenge of carrying your body. It is a great gift for someone to agree to be your pallbearer, but a gift is not something you should expect or even demand. It's always wise to be gentle with people, especially with topics and choices such as these.

WHO DO YOU WANT TO SERVE AS PALLBEARERS?

_____

_____

ALL MADE UP AND NOWHERE TO GO

For all you girls (and wannabe girls), it's a good idea to write down all the makeup products you use and how you use them. Make sure you have everything in stock at all times because you just never know when you'll need them. You don't want all your friends and family members at your visitation to wander frantically around the funeral home or house of worship and miss the festivities because they can't find a corpse that looks like you. (Perhaps one of them sort of looked like you, but they weren't sure because it looked more like a drag queen or a clown.) Think about those times when you tried to get your makeup done at department stores, thinking you were going to come out looking like Angelina Jolie and instead, $600 later, you came out looking like a Vegas showgirl meant to look good ten rows back. Can you say "too much rouge?" Be prepared.

On the other hand, if you've always had a fantasy of looking like someone else— Princess Di, Paris Hilton, George Clooney, or even Al Gore—this is your last chance for your friends and loved ones to see you as you've always (sort of) wanted to be seen.

Before the revolution of 1921 in Mongolia, death practices there were unique, to say the least. Immediately after death, the face was covered. (There is a Mongolian proverb: "In life cover your private parts, in death your face.") It was forbidden to look upon or touch the corpse, especially the face. If the eyes or the mouth weren't closed, only a close male relative or a lama (holy man) could close them. In certain areas of the country, after the corpse was transported to the funeral site on horseback, the horse was made to gallop. When the corpse was thrown off, that place would become the actual burial site.

YOU CAN TAKE
IT WITH YOU
WHEN YOU GO

Our motto—have fun with it! What about your tennis racket, your iPod loaded with your favorite songs, a beloved kitchen utensil, a musical instrument, a whip (don't ask), a photo of your pet, a rock or special shell, a favorite toy from your childhood, a book that inspired you, your TV remote control (you could be holding it with a little sign that says, FINALLY, IT'S ALL MINE!), those carved wooden hands from the 1960s giving people the finger, an old Christmas ornament, a photo of your secret love, a political button, your winning lottery ticket (a copy, of course), a favorite comic book, a PlayStation, lucky dice or poker chips, a deck of cards, or a beautiful paperweight from your collection? How about a bumper sticker on your coffin: I'D REALLY RATHER BE IN PHILADELPHIA! or "BODY ON BOARD!" or "HEAVEN DOESN'T WANT ME, HELL IS AFRAID I'LL TAKE OVER" or "HAVE A NICE DAY!" (with a little rainbow or smiley face). The possibilities are endless.

It is estimated by the Centers for Disease Control (CDC) that bubonic plague, commonly called the Black Death, has killed approximately 300 million people from the first known case in the 11th century BC to the most recent account in 2007.

ARE THERE ANY PERSONAL MEMENTOES YOU WISH TO HAVE WITH YOU INSIDE YOUR COFFIN?

_____

_____

_____

There's no better time than now to start looking for or at least thinking about your burial place. Another Buyer Beware: Sometimes when buying a plot in a cemetery, they will show you a sample plot and not the one you actually will be getting. It's kind of like a "show apartment" in a new building. Be sure to ask to be taken to the exact plot location. We suggest drawing a little map or bringing your GPS with you whenever shopping for plots.

You might want to seek out a haunted cemetery—just think of the interesting conversations you can have with revolutionary soldiers or a famous writer! If you do want to haunt, you better have someone entertaining there to haunt with!

Today many people move around throughout their lives. If that's true for you and you're worried about buying a plot in advance, there may be a solution. Many cemeteries now belong to credit exchange programs, which allow for a dollar-for-dollar transfer of services and merchandise between participating cemeteries. When prearranging, be sure to ask your local provider about exchange privileges offered.

WHERE DO YOU WANT TO BE BURIED?

_____

_____

Did you ever imagine there could be so many choices involved with a traditional burial? That's one of the reasons we think it's so important and such a great gift to your loved ones to make these decisions in advance, when you're feeling good and/or up to the task. To paraphrase Woody Allen: on the plus side of traditional burial, it's one of the few things that can be done easily lying down. So at least it's got that going for it! Even then, this is absolutely not the lazy man's way out. It takes some effort to get it right, but you're worth it!

MORE THOUGHTS ON A TRADITIONAL BURIAL:

_____

_____

_____

_____

_____

_____

_____

_____

_____

_____

_____

_____

_____

_____

_____

_____

_____

_____

_____

_____

_____

_____

The Declaration of Independence was signed around one o'clock on July 4, 1776. Fifty years later, on July 4, 1826, Thomas Jefferson died at almost exactly the same time. A few hours later, Jefferson's good friend and cosigner, John Adams, died. His last words were "Thomas Jefferson still survives." Who knew?!

CHAPTER 5

GREEN BURIAL

GRAVE PASTURES

Dear reader, we want you to know that "green" burials, also known as "natural" burials, are becoming very popular—they're not just for survivalists, commune members, and mobsters. Regular folks choose them, too! People are concerned about the Earth (well, not everyone, unfortunately), and out of that concern comes a strong interest in green burials. Everyone, from an eighty-five-year-old southern lady to a twenty-seven-year-old Web millionaire, is doing the green grave thing!

Natural burial is as old as death itself. It shows great respect for the Earth from which we all came. Green burial avoids preservative chemicals, steel, and concrete tombs that are designed to

Each year, 22,500 cemeteries across the United States bury approximately:

30 million board feet of hardwood (caskets)
104,272 tons of steel (caskets and vaults)
2,700 tons of copper and bronze (caskets)
1,636,000 tons of reinforced concrete (vaults)
827,060 gallons of embalming fluid, which most commonly includes formaldehyde. (It is worth noting that embalming fluid chemically changes in the act of preserving the body and is not largely present as a fluid, so this figure refers to embalming fluid before it is introduced to the body.)

Natural burial grounds in the United States

❖ Cedar Brook Burial Ground, Limington, Maine
❖ Eternal Rest Memories Park, Dunedin, Florida
❖ Ethician Family Burial Ground, San Jacinto County, Texas
❖ Forever Fernwood, Mill Valley, California
❖ Glendale Memorial Nature Preserve, DeFuniak Springs, Florida
❖ Greensprings, Newfield, New York
❖ Honey Creek Woodlands, Conyers, Georgia
❖ Ramsey Creek Preserve, Westminster, South Carolina
❖ The Commonweal Conservancy, Santa Fe, New Mexico

keep your body from decomposing naturally. This method ensures the burial site remains as natural as possible in all respects. Embalming fluid is not used, and the body is interred in a biodegradable casket—wood, cardboard, paper, wicker, or untreated bamboo. No endangered tropical woods or plastic are allowed. The body is wrapped in a simple shroud, perhaps a favorite blanket or quilt. Remember, you cannot use artificial fabrics such as polyester, acrylic, or spandex. Of course if you want to look slim and alluring for the viewing, you might want to rethink the green burial so you can wear that full body spandex suit to smooth out the bumps and make you look ten pounds slimmer. (So much for the green burial for us!)

A recent AARP website poll queried: "Which type of burial is most appealing?" Only 8 percent responded with a traditional cemetery burial, and a mere 18 percent opted for cremation. A whopping 70.4 percent chose green burial. AARP claims over 38 million members, all fifty years of age or older, making it one of the largest and most powerful organizations in the United States. It has a terrific website for information on funerals, burials, and related consumer issues. Check it out.

At the beginning of 2008, there were only nine cemeteries in the United States that declared themselves as completely green. However, more are being developed every day. In addition, many conventional cemeteries are working to incorporate green burials into their establishments. If you do not have a green facility in your area, you can check with your local cemeteries to see if they allow green or natural burials. Most conventional cemeteries require a coffin with an indestructible lining, and although they don't require embalming, they do encourage it.

Besides limiting the amount of chemicals used in a conventional burial, the green movement is also about land conservation and preservation of open spaces, which can foster multiple uses. Proponents of green burial envision preserving millions of acres that look and feel like natural parks, even though they are actually burial grounds. Presently all of the green cemeteries are land trusts and will never be developed.

What we call "conventional burial" is actually a relatively recent tradition. It wasn't that long ago that all burials were green or natural. Green burials are what the pilgrims and the pioneers did. Most of what we think of today as the traditional funeral—embalming, expensive caskets, manicured cemeteries—are practices that began in the late 1800s when burying the dead became an industry.

The Civil War totally changed the way Americans cared for their dead. For centuries, families had prepared their deceased at home—cleaning, dressing, and burying them in the family cemetery. Most people abhorred any unnatural intervention into the body's organic processes of decomposition. In fact, they felt that embalming was blasphemous, breaking from the Biblical tradition of "ashes to ashes, dust to dust." During the Civil War, more than 600,000 people died, and doctors began embalming the corpses and placing them in sturdy coffins so they could endure the long trips home from the battlefields. Even then, some considered the doctors to be sinful for tampering with the corpses.

In 1868 federal legislation required that each state keep a registry of deaths through reporting from health and religious officials. The government passed this legislation in response to the trauma of the Civil War, in which no reliable records were available for tens of thousands of soldiers who were killed.

Princess Diana is buried on a small island on the grounds of her family estate, Althorp. Her interment drew attention to the idea of being buried at home, but before you start digging up the backyard, be aware that having a dead body under the rhododendrons can lessen the value of your home by 25 percent—at least in the United Kingdom.

With a natural burial you are doing a great service to the planet, but you are also doing a great thing for your wallet. It's nice when those two things match up. The average traditional funeral costs about $6,500 for the service, a coffin, and other ancillary items. Plus it's not unusual to pay an additional $3,500 for the plot and burial—bringing the total to around $10,000 for a conventional funeral with burial.

Green burials can range anywhere between $1,000 and $10,000, although the cost generally tends to be much lower than a traditional burial. Some green cemeteries do not actually charge for the privilege of being buried in their beautiful spaces, but they take contributions, which go to land trusts and are tax deductible. As with standard funerals, always be sure to discuss any financial questions in advance with the facility. (We love that Glendale Memorial Nature Preserve takes PayPal for the funeral and burial costs.)

Now let's move on to the fun part—like choosing the biodegradable casket, your wardrobe, your shroud/blanket/quilt, flowers, plants, and grave markers. You know—the creative stuff!

Don't worry. You can still have very lively, colorful, energetic, even drunken green burials. You don't need to be a vegetarian or a PETA member. Tell them what you want. Lay it all out, kind of like laying out your body; it's unmistakably you! And a reminder—by providing this information, you are doing your family a great service.

If you decide you want to have a green burial, the next most important decision is where your final resting place will be. If you decide to get buried on family land and it's legal in your area, keep in mind that your family may not live there forever and therefore no one may be there to tend your plot. In some states, you can get an easement on any future sales of your property that guarantees your little graveyard will be protected. In other states, graveyards of all sorts automatically get an easement. Check with your state and local government about rules and regulations on natural graveyards outside the established cemeteries. A highly respected expert in the field of do-it-yourself burials is Lisa Carlson, whose book *Caring For the Dead: Your Final Act of Love* we recommend if considering home burial in nonofficial areas. The Funeral Consumers Alliance website (www.funerals.org) also gives state-by-state information on home burial—just go to the section: "Caring For Your Own Dead."

We recommend being open to traveling great distances or even out of state if a true green burial is your desire. Since there are so few green burial sites at this time, you may want to go to the effort (or rather have your family make the effort) to travel. You can talk to your local funeral director about transporting the body, or you may just want to do it yourself. (*Little Miss Sunshine* comes to mind.) Just make sure you stock up on dry ice so the body won't deteriorate. Don't forget the body bag! We don't think Zip-Lock makes 'em that big. You can call a funeral home or hospital to see if they will sell you one. Or—like other miracles on the Internet, you can buy body bags direct. Just google "Transport Pouches." We've seen them range from $25 to $45. You can also find them on eBay, and then you'll be able to use PayPal. But of course this might not be the most prudent time to participate in a long auction to save a few dollars—"I've only got twenty-three hours left and I can save five dollars!" Meanwhile, Mom's "resting" in the freezer.

We might be tempted to say don't worry about crossing state lines unless you're smuggling drugs in your coffin, but we would be wrong. You do have to look into the state laws about interstate transport of dead bodies. Many states only allow it if the deceased is embalmed.

Another factor to consider in your choice of location: how far will your family want to travel if they care to visit your grave in the upcoming years? Remember that legally the deceased can only advise or

Attributed to the Buddha at his death: "Recognize that all that lives is subject to the laws of impermanence, and strive for eternal wisdom."

request what they want to do after death. The family may not want to travel so far to visit your grave, so they can pretty much do what they want once you're gone. Doesn't sound fair, does it? You're the one who's been dragging this thing around for years—like your whole life—and they're going to tell you what to do with it now?

You and your family may want to "scout the location," like for a movie. This will be the final, climactic scene of your life, so don't be hasty. You may have a variety of terrains from which to choose: a mountain overlooking a valley or another mountain; alongside a river, pond, or ocean; in an open expanse of green fields; or in the middle of a forest. They're building a natural cemetery in Santa Fe, New Mexico, so you could even select a desert location in the future. Just be sure to have someone take you to the exact location of your final plot.

At this juncture, we want to coin a new term for *grave* and *plot*. All through this book we've been struggling with those words: *grave* is just too sad and there's nothing fun about it at all; *plot* sounds like you're out to assassinate or murder someone. We don't think that association is unintentional. Now, get ready for a revolutionary new way we'll talk and therefore think about where your body ends up (drum roll, please)—it shall forevermore be known as the *B-spot*—for the body-spot! Get it? The riff on the G-spot is absolutely intentional. It's the climax of your life.

So, in selecting your B-spot, keep in mind that some of the green cemeteries don't have roads, and none of them allow upright stone markers. Most

In a Tibetan "sky burial," no fuel, land, or topsoil are consumed. Tibetans believe in reincarnation and feel no need to preserve the body once the soul has gone. After death, there is a period of three days for mourning and prayers. Then the corpse is cut into pieces and put on a mountaintop. In just minutes the body may be picked free of all flesh by vultures. Tibetans believe they are helping to perpetuate life through this offering of the body.

likely your site will be overgrown with vegetation, so you will be encouraged to use a GPS device to enable your family and friends to find your B-spot when they feel like communing with your spirit.

You may be wondering—can't a bear, wolf, or other large animal (your estranged brother-in-law, for example) dig down, get your body, and devour it? In the experience of all nine green burial cemeteries/nature preserves (as of this writing), they have never heard of any animals disturbing a gravesite. If you're a worrywart, you're going to assume that it just hasn't happened yet, and if you're an optimist, you'll be relieved at the thought of your B-spot being safe and sound.

Almost all conventional pet cemeteries are separate from human cemeteries. However, green cemeteries have broken with that tradition, and some allow beloved pets to be buried in the family plot. In East Texas at the Ethician Family Cemetery, not only are people encouraged to use their plots for pets, there are even provisions for "sky burials" for large pets such as horses, elephants, or tigers.

WHERE DO YOU WANT YOUR GREEN BURIAL TO BE?

_____

_____

DO YOU WANT TO BE BURIED IN A COFFIN? IF SO, WHAT KIND?

_____

_____

DO YOU WANT TO BE BURIED WITH YOUR PET(S)?
ANY SPECIAL REQUESTS?

_____

_____

As we said earlier, if you want to be buried in a coffin, your only choices are wood, cardboard, paper, wicker, or untreated bamboo. These can be painted or covered in cloth or other natural materials, as long as biodegradable paints and glues are being used. Most natural cemeteries prefer no use of endangered tropical woods. Plywood and chipboard are not allowed because of the way they're processed. If you love high fashion or you're color crazy, you might want to shop around for or commission well-designed pine or cardboard coffins that have some artwork on them. No fears of copyright infringement here—go ahead and make it a Louis Vuitton–covered coffin. They can't sue you; the artwork won't be above ground for long, and besides, you'll be dead!

We have found that some of the most stunning cardboard coffins come from the United Kingdom and Australia. The Ecopod—a recycled paper coffin based on the shape of an Egyptian sarcophagus—comes from England and is beginning to be distributed in the United States. It's sleek and almost futuristic looking and comes in various colors with a choice of designs. There is a gold-leaf model with an option for cream or blue feathers on the inside. But as far as the highly decorated cardboard models go, it's well worth the effort to do some research about these designs, because if you can't afford to ship from those countries, you may be able to borrow some of their ideas.

We're sure that once this catches on, all sorts of artists will want to make designer coffins—no kidding. The brave ones will want to participate in celebrating the lives of their customers in death as they have in life. Imagine Ralph Lauren doing a Western-themed coffin using beautifully weathered reclaimed barn wood with inlaid turquoise. Prada is using lots of feathers in their designs right now—imagine a soft-shaped pod covered in beautiful ostrich feathers, like a lovely bird gently landing on the earth. Mario Buatta could design a chintz- or velvet-covered coffin, or perhaps a custom made toile with scenes from your life. This could also become a matching shroud. Afterwards, your family can have pillows, curtains, bedspreads, placemats, or throws made of the same fabric to remember you by.

In the movie business, when you see an actor getting hit over the head with a bottle and it smashes, such bottles are made of sugar. Why not create a kind of Sleeping Beauty coffin made mostly of wood or cardboard, but with a warm-tinted sugar glass "window" over your "sleeping" face? Of course you can only do this if you are having a speedy burial because there can be no embalming. But if you're already interested in green burials, you're on the cutting edge. So carry that thinking over to the design of the casket as well.

If you can paint, then you can design your own coffin. Actually, even if you can't paint, you can decorate your own coffin or, better yet, let your friends and family do it. Think about it as a big plaster cast for a broken arm or leg. Remember how thrilling it was when you were a kid and people began to write encouragements, funny poems, jokes, crazy sayings, or just their names on

> The Vietnamese believe that their dead must be buried in their homeland, or the soul will wander aimlessly in pain and suffering. Family members wash the unembalmed body and dress it in the best clothes. The body is wedged into an elaborate wooden coffin with reed branches, paper, and other objects to keep it in place. After three years, the deceased's family will dig up the body, cleanse the skeleton, rebury the remains, or put them into a "bone jar" and keep them on the family altar.

your cast? Unlike a broken bone, this healing is going to take place in the afterlife. You can even make or buy stencils with stars and moons and dogs and cats or just about anything you can imagine.

This can be a very therapeutic activity for your friends and family—or you, if you're doing it in advance as we have advised. Think about buying a coffin ahead of time—and when you get together with your family, pull out the coffin, add to it, and embellish it; make it a family tradition. (It could make for the centerpiece of one hell of a family reunion!) With a cast, the good wishes are there to help you heal; with a coffin, the good wishes are there to heal the ones left behind. If you're doing this for someone else, this can also help to focus on celebrating the person's life and ease some of the sorrow that goes with his or her passing. Write all about Grandpa's children and grandchildren and how much love he's leaving behind. Go ahead and paint their life story, perhaps with a timeline. Here's an example:

Carmen Eva Flowers—loved to laugh, loved her third husband Vern madly, loved to travel, loved her dogs, loved white chocolate, loved her friends, she saw the ridiculous in life and embraced it.

And here's another:

Sue Anne (still doesn't like her middle name) Bailey—was born into a family of five children with two parents. She was child number four and was supposed to be the last one, but her brother Bruce had to come along and ruin it all. Well, not exactly. She did well overall, although it was rough going for the first eighty-five [or whatever] years. She had no children but loved her cats dearly (like many crazy old ladies, but it began when she was young)—starting with her cat Romeo, who came into her life when she was eight years old. He saved her life from the craziness to come, because she had someone to love who loved her back. (Yada Yada Yada. You get the idea . . .)

These are examples of what we would say on our personalized coffins. Next comes a chance for family and friends to add their thoughts and sentiments This whole idea made us eager to get our coffins in advance to start the decorating process.

WRITINGS/DRAWINGS YOU MAY WANT ON YOUR COFFIN:

_____
_____
_____
_____
_____
_____

WHAT TO WEAR WHEN YOU'RE GOING UNDER

All of the green cemeteries allow you to be buried in a shroud, quilt, afghan, or blanket—without a coffin. You can also wear clothes underneath the covering. Some cemeteries allow burial without a coffin, but you need to check with each one. Cotton and wool are the most popular fabrics to be buried in, but also consider silk, hemp, bamboo, or even soy jersey (who knew?). Any organic cloth will work—just watch out for items like plastic buttons, metal zippers, polyester thread, girl scout insignias, or AA pins.

Again, be creative and go out with some flourish. Use this as an avenue of self-expression. We're talking about your life, after all. Think of the possibilities for a gorgeous shroud in rich colors and patterns using organic cotton, silk, or cashmere. Why not a Michael Kors–designed cashmere knit body bag, a flag if you're a veteran, denim if you're a cowgirl, African Kente cloth, embroidered Indian silk, camouflage fabric if you're a survivalist, deerskin with a beaded Native American design, fluorescent orange if you're a hunter (don't worry about getting shot—you're already dead!), or your family's tartan if you're Scottish? Leave everyone wanting more. Nature isn't black and white, so why do you have to be? Go out in the true natural and colorful style. Environmentally conscious doesn't mean boring.

Choosing or designing a shroud, quilt, or blanket can be the beginning of a new

Canada and the United States are the only two nations that regularly practice the ancient art of embalming. National Cancer Institute studies have found that anatomists and embalmers, professions with high exposure to formaldehyde, are at an increased risk for brain and colon cancer as well as leukemia. Additionally, casket manufacturers are listed as one of the Environmental Protection Agency's top fifty hazardous waste generators, due to chemicals such as methyl and xylene used in the protective finish sprayed on the exteriors of caskets.

Many people in Madagascar practice famadihana—or turning over of the dead (literally)—a ritual in which people exhume and rebury their deceased family members. Generally this ritual takes place every five to seven years, when a family member has a dream that a dead relative complains that he or she is cold in the tomb. Once the body is exhumed, whatever remains is rewrapped in a new shroud. The celebrants parade their ancestors through town to show them what has changed since the last time they were buried.

family tradition (better than picking on one of your younger siblings during the holidays). Think about the AIDS Memorial Quilt, created in 1987. People came together to commemorate their loved ones by creating individual panels reflecting their lives. It continues to grow today, panel-by-panel, as people use handmade appliqués, collages, iron-on transfers, paint, buttons, and various insignias.

If you know good seamstresses, weavers, quilters, or knitters, why not have your own personalized shroud made? Let the whole family contribute. Or not. You can start by gathering cloth that has personal meaning—a silk scarf that Grandma wore on her first trip to Paris, part of the hem of Mom's wedding dress, a pillowcase Dad lifted from his favorite hotel, a cut from your bris outfit, or a square of your first communion dress. You can even take pieces from the clothes your uncle or husband wore at his funeral. Just remember to get it before the funeral directors have their way with it. Your uncle won't miss a patch from the back of his jacket or his shirt if he's dead. Ask your aunt for one of her old pullovers while she's still alive. Maybe when your mom isn't looking, cut a strip from her old, ratty bathrobe. Better yet, tear it up and make it look like the dog did it.

A simple cotton sheet, a swath of silk, or a few yards of linen may be turned into a poignant memory blanket. You can buy small silk pouches with drawstring openings on wedding paraphernalia websites (another example of the yin and yang of funerals and weddings) and fill them with all kinds of mementos, such as dried flowers, herbs or tea, corn kernels or lentils, a favorite candy, seeds, feathers, some fur from your pet, small photos, locks of hair, fake eyelashes, antacids, stamps, tiny rocks, shells, a fresh cigarette, marijuana, antidepressants, candies, semiprecious stone beads, or leaves or bark from the deceased's favorite trees. Or fill the bags with small pieces of paper on which you or your family and friends have written jokes, song lyrics, poems, literary passages, prayers, recipes, movie lines, a passage from a favorite book, a page from your travel journal, a lottery ticket, or a letter admitting you to a prestigious college. Sew or glue the pouches onto the fabric, and you'll have a powerful and meaningful shroud that reminds you of the richness of your life.

Maybe you'd like to have a life-size picture of you silk-screened onto some cotton or a large piece of linen and turned into a shroud. Just make sure you use biodegradable paint or natural plant dyes. Have a montage of your life silk-screened onto your biodegradable fabric, using various photos from your life as you grew up. Make it a shroud about you and your passions, interests, and loves. Don't limit it to artwork. Have everyone write their feelings about you, a story about you, a shared experience, your test results, prayers for you, or perhaps their favorite memories of you. Write prayers all over the entire fabric. Attach special pieces of clothing to it such as Grandpa's stained barbeque apron or Dad's favorite plaid hunting jacket. Imagine Mom's beautiful monogrammed hand towel placed right in the middle—perhaps with her photo silk-screened on it. The final product can take on the look of a beautiful, artistic collage. Again—use biodegradable glue if you can't sew. (Hint: Glue guns are very handy!) Glue on some of your mom's rickrack or vintage ribbon. If you want, you can choose to be clothed under the shroud, so we urge you to choose an outfit you loved or looked thin in or that reminds you of the best day of your life.

If you're lucky enough to know how to knit or crochet or weave, the sky's the limit for your final cover. Have fun but choose your colors thoughtfully. Reaction to color

The techniques of dying used by yogis are very methodical, painless, and conscious. One traditional way for certain Himalayan yogis to move to the next realm is to sit in meditation, enter the state of consciousness called samadhi, and allow the body to freeze in the cold mountain air. Another extremely rare technique entails meditating on the solar plexus in a way that generates great internal heat, which induces spontaneous combustion of the body.

Hindus believe that once the soul has shed the body, the corpse must be disposed of as soon as practicable. Then the soul won't be tempted to linger and will continue on its karmic journey. Hindus also believe that by dying in Benares (now Varanasi) on the Ganges River, it helps to break the cycle of death and rebirth. There are eighty funeral pyres along the river for cremation in this holy city. Often, people are unable to cremate their loved ones and will simply float the bodies down the river instead.

is almost instantaneous and visceral—and at a time like this, people are primed to experience things even more intensely. There is a field of psychology devoted to analyzing the effect of color on human behavior and feelings. Colors can create physical reactions, so use this to effect. Red has been shown to raise blood pressure and increase enthusiasm (She was wonderful, so beautiful, I loved her—Mother Theresa and Sofia Loren all rolled into one!), while the colors blue and green can make a person calm and peaceful. Yellow shines with optimism (Maybe they're not dead!), enlightenment, and happiness (Yes! I'll never have to work again!), and brown connects us to the earth, (which is where you'll end up.) There are lots of books available on the power and significance of color that you might want to look at when you're planning your design. Did you ever think you would be able to say so much when you're dead? You can weave the story of your life and have it end any way you want, for instance, "I wasn't a jerk, after all!"

The only problem with being buried in quilts is that they're so beautiful and many of them are irreplaceable and priceless. Of course, so are you. They're almost historic artifacts (which is what you will become). Instead of using an heirloom quilt, we suggest getting a new one and adding your own history to it. However, this is your sendoff, so if you want to celebrate your life by being wrapped in your grandmother's quilt, then we wholeheartedly endorse it. Don't let us make you feel guilty. That's not our intent. Also, try going on eBay where you can find exquisite, unusual, and affordable quilts rather easily. Or go online and get inexpensive, dazzling quilts from India—just watch out for metallic decoration and nonbiodegradable fabrics.

WHAT KIND OF SHROUD OR COVERING DO YOU WANT
FOR YOUR GREEN BURIAL?

_____

_____

YOUR GREEN GRAVE MARKER

You need to check with your cemetery about grave markers. Some allow locally found flat rocks that can be engraved, survey markers in brass or aluminum, native plants, nursery plants, and trees. Most do not allow invasive plants like kudzu or purple loosestrife that can strangle a live person overnight. If you're from the South you'll know what we're talking about. Just imagine being in bed when a large leafed kudzu vine pushes itself through your open window and winds itself around your neck. It's been known to completely cover a cow in eight hours.

The people who work at the cemetery can help you with any plant decision you're grappling with. They might even steer you to some fabulous greenery you've never even heard of. This is going to be the last image that everyone will have of you and, in some cases, will continue to have of you (imagine your family coming back every year and cutting a flower or a branch from a bush or tree that they planted on your B-Spot). If you are a great gardener or love having fresh flowers around your home, then go wild with them at your

At Glendale Memorial Nature Preserve in Glendale, Florida, there are only 30 to 100 burials per acre. Contemporary cemeteries typically bury between 800 to 3,000 people per acre.

A ten-acre swatch of typical, nongreen cemetery ground will contain enough coffin wood to construct more than forty homes, nearly a thousand tons of casket steel, and another twenty thousand tons of concrete for vaults. Across North America, enough metal is diverted into coffin and vault production annually to build the Golden Gate Bridge every year, and enough concrete is used to build a two-lane highway from New York to Detroit.

burial. You can scatter your favorites around the perimeter of your B-Spot. Think about a crown of rosemary on your head for remembrance or a lei of orchids for love and beauty. Visualize being buried wrapped in a long garland of flowers or plants.

You don't have to go crazy trying to find the symbolism of different trees, plants, flowers, and bushes, but this is your last appearance so we suggest that you make the best of it and do a bit of research. For instance, bamboo means longevity—perhaps not the greatest message at this time—but it also means strength and grace and symbolizes the path toward enlightenment, which we think is rather beautiful.

YOUR FLORAL FINALE

With regard to flowers, be sure to think about the flowers that are blooming in the different seasons, and choose ones for each time of the year—because you probably won't know when you're going to die. (Have you ever noticed when newly dead people are depicted in cartoons, they always hold a bouquet of daisies? And then our favorite theme: women at weddings carry bouquets of flowers—funerals and weddings being so similar and connected in the subconscious.) Think outside of the normal flower box—go beyond the typical funeral flowers and include plants and trees of all kinds. Envision your friends throwing masses of rose petals or seeds or golden leaves into your grave on a frosty fall day. Perhaps they would lay down boughs of balsam pine across your B-spot. Consider the different smells, shapes, and colors that you like—juniper branches, magnolia leaves, peony bushes, daffodils, whole tobacco leaves, tulips, pussy wil-

Jews and Muslims have always practiced ecological burial customs, and they share many similarities in the way they bury their dead. Both do not embalm or cremate, nor do they have viewings. In their homelands they never use a casket. However, in the United States Jews use a plain pine box. Both place the body in a simple shroud and both must bury their dead as soon as possible.

lows, hydrangeas, rosemary, eucalyptus, black-eyed Susans, or cabbage flowers. Expand that concept to include all natural materials like pine cones, bark, driftwood, mosses, cattails, ferns, shells (if allowed), rocks, bare limbs, mushrooms, birds' nests, hornets' nests (better be empty and inactive—but then again, think of that crazy brother-in-law), oyster fungus, a small animal skull, seed pods, or a pile of pine needles.

You should check out the artist Andy Goldsworthy for inspiration in using nature to create beautiful works of art for your B-spot. He's world renowned for using leaves, ice, branches, rocks, pebbles, logs, limbs, sticks, and whatever else is available to create totally unique works of art, both modern and ancient in effect. With the permission of your chosen cemetery, you can go as far as you like in creating an impermanent temple of sorts. If we had our choice, we would love an Andy Goldsworthy type of creation to commemorate us. Here's the catch—you need to get the agreement of the people carrying out your wishes—or get them to hire a local artist or gardener to help.

Remember: simple always works and something unique can be done rather easily—so it seems to us that people would honor your request if you wanted a

Sun Bear, a Chippewa medicine man, explains how Native Americans used to die:

"In the old way, when it was time to die, old ones would go off by themselves, feeling that the moment of death was as intimate between them and the Earth Mother as the moment of birth is between human mother and child. They would find a quiet place and there make prayers to the Great Spirit, thanking him for the life they had enjoyed. They would sing their song, and they would die."

simple and unusual display of any sort.

Of course, if your cemetery allows, one of the best things you can do is to plant a tree, bush, or bulbs on your grave—for its permanence and for the giving back to the Earth. What better symbol than that?

A postscript: There were a few years when Carmen lost several close friends and during that period her godmother, Didi, created a lovely tradition. With each death she gave Carmen a young flowering tree to plant in memory of them. Carmen would watch the trees grow and blossom and would feel close to her friends over the years. It was so comforting that she still feels the love in that gesture. Similarly, Sue gave two young hydrangea bushes to her friend Kathy each time one of her parents died. Kathy loves to think of her parents as the bushes grow and blossom over the years. Tell your friends if you'd like to be remembered in this way. (If you're sweet and dangerous, a blackberry bush or raspberry bush might be perfect—thorny yet delicious!)

MORE THOUGHTS ON GREEN BURIAL:

_____
_____
_____
_____
_____
_____
_____
_____
_____
_____
_____
_____
_____
_____
_____
_____
_____
_____
_____
_____
_____
_____
_____
_____
_____
_____
_____
_____
_____
_____
_____
_____
_____
_____
_____

CHAPTER 6

BODY DONATION AND CREMATION

IT WON'T COST YOU AN ARM AND A LEG, SO TO SPEAK

Okay, we've covered traditional and green burials, now for the fun stuff. Not that those other forms of dealing with the body can't be fun and creative, but we think you know by now the possibilities are endless. And we predict those possibilities will continue to grow, as people begin to get over their fears of facing the end.

We'd bet that most of you have never heard of some of the new ways in which to dispose of the body, or "gift" it back to the Earth, or change it into a form that you can carry with you at all times.

Your head will spin with all the choices—unless you freeze it for $50,000 just in case scientists can clone you in the distant future so you can come back the same wonderful self you always were. Who knew? The fun has just begun in the wonderful world of alternative body disposal.

We're starting this chapter on a serious note—body and organ donation. Stay with us here because we've been so fascinated by our research that we've decided to donate our bodies—or at least our organs—when we die.

Let's start with body donation. You've heard all the crazy stories about donated bodies being used as crash test dummies, placed outside in a field in Tennessee to observe how corpses decompose, and human spines being sold on the black market. Well, we're here to tell you that all of it is true, but that shouldn't prevent you from considering the fact that you can help improve and even save the lives of as many as twenty-five to fifty individuals because of your organ donations. In addition, consider how many others you could benefit through medical research and education. We want bargain shoppers to be aware that you'll get a free cremation down the line. (Have you ever turned down anything free in your life?) And think about all the animal testing you can prevent by donating your body and/or organs.

We know that a lot of people are afraid that their dead body would be ridiculed and mistreated by some medical student. (Is that any different from visits to the doctor in our daily lives?) Well, Carmen went to nursing school and had her own cadaver, which she named Clarence. She has never seen anything treated with such tenderness and appreciation by so many people—the cadavers were revered. After the cadavers had been used to teach surgery, orthopedics, ophthalmology, cardiology, neurology, and other specialty fields, the medical school cremated the bodies. Many of the students attended the cremation, said prayers, and gave thanks to the souls for the enormous help in their education. The ashes were always returned at the families' requests.

If you're feeling a little queasy about whole body donation, or if you have big plans for an open casket funeral, we have two words for you—organ donation. Nearly one hundred thousand men, women, and children are currently awaiting organ and tissue transplants, yet there were only twelve thousand organ and body donors in 2007. We think this is collective insanity! Either that, or people are just not thinking about it. You can directly save the lives of many people when you make the decision to become an organ and/or tissue donor.

Often, families deny organ donation at the time of death because they think it is against their religion, but in reality most religions support organ donation. Some families are worried that the body will be mutilated and they won't be able to have an open coffin visitation. That won't be the case, since donated organs are removed surgically in a routine operation similar to gallbladder or appendix removal. If you are embalmed, they remove your organs anyway—sometimes putting them in a little bag at your feet (Hmm . . . save a life, or keep that little bag close by? The choice is easy for us.) Many organizations have no age limit for organ and tissue donation; of course this depends on the physical condition of the donor. Some medical schools require that a donor register before death; however, in many cases, next-of-kin may make the bequest without prior arrangement.

In a macabre turn of medical marketing, body brokers are now connecting wealthy patients with healthy but poor people willing to sell their organs for cash. The international market for human parts is thriving: a kidney goes for $25,000 in Russia, a heart for $290,000 in South Africa. Sound expensive? It's often a fraction of the cost of surgery in the United States—and delivery takes weeks instead of years. For the biggest inventory, head to China, where many organs available for transplant are harvested from executed prisoners—a practice the government says it's trying to end.

DO YOU WANT TO DONATE YOUR BODY TO MEDICAL RESEARCH?
IF SO, WHERE DO YOU WANT IT TO GO?

_____

_____

_____

DO YOU WANT TO DONATE ORGANS? IF SO, WHICH ONES?
HOW ABOUT ALL OF THEM?

_____

_____

_____

Nowadays there are so many types of organs, tissues, and stem cells that may be used or transplanted and put to good use. Go to www.OrganDonor.gov for more information. Be aware that only your family can give the okay for your body or organ donation, regardless of what your driver's license says, so make sure they know and understand your wishes. Tell them now!

CREMATION: OUT OF THE GRAVE INTO THE PYRE

Cremation is fast becoming the predominant way Americans dispose of their bodies, but it's truly only been around in modern times for over a century. Ancient cultures burned their dead for thousands of years, but the early Christians shunned cremation, thinking it pagan and antithetical to their belief in resurrection. They also followed the Jewish tradition of entombment and burial. Once Emperor Constantine christianized the Holy Roman Empire in 400 A.D., the Christian method of burial essentially became the only way in Western civilization, except during times of war and plague. In modern times, the pope did not sanction cremation until 1963.

Today, cremation is the practice of disposing of a human corpse by burning it at a temperature between 1,400 and 2,100 degrees Fahrenheit. In 2005, out of 2,432,000 deaths in the United States, approximately 31 percent, or a total of 778,000 people, chose to be cremated. U.S. cremation statistics project that the number will rise to more than 50 percent by 2025. In the United Kingdom, approximately 70 percent of the population is cremated, heavily influenced by the lack of space on their island. Interestingly, in 2005 Nevada had

Most scholars agree that cremation probably began in the early Stone Age around 3000 B.C. Due to the rise of Christianity, by 400 A.D., earth burial replaced cremation. In 1873, Queen Victoria recommended cremation for health and hygiene reasons but was met with opposition from the Anglican Church and the British government. Cremation was forced into law ten years later when a Welsh doctor, William Price, burned his son named Jesus Christ in a pagan ritual. Dr. Price was tried in an 1884 court case that resulted in an amendment to legalize the process.

the highest rate of cremation in the United States at 65 percent. Perhaps this has something to do with all those gamblers having heart attacks and being unable to get home properly. Also, they've lost all their money and can't afford a traditional burial—and you know they didn't plan ahead for one. Of course they mostly don't plan ahead for getting married in that state either, hence all those little wedding chapels in people's garages. We're wondering—do they have lots of backyard crematoriums in Nevada and drive-in funeral parlors? And why is it that on the Google/Nevada funeral home page, right in the middle of all the Nevada funeral directors and funeral homes search sites, there's a $120/hour escort service website? Maybe you need a trick if you've lost all your money and buried your best friend—lucky you saved that last $120!

In January 1656, a Spanish soldier arrived in Naples and was admitted to a hospital. The doctor quickly diagnosed the Black Death symptoms and reported them to the government. Unfortunately, the viceroy wasn't keen on bad news and did not take any action, and the plague broke out. In one week, approximately 60,000 people were cremated. By the end of the outbreak in May, it had killed half of the city's 300,000 inhabitants.

Today there is some controversy about the environmental impact of cremation. The key issues are its heavy use of fossil fuel energy to burn a body for two to three hours and mercury emissions from old silver dental fillings. Just how much damage is done to the environment is highly debatable. What we do know is that in terms of land use, cremation is more green than traditional burial. Compare a huge metal or wooden coffin slowly disintegrating over decades, leaking all sorts of horrible toxins into the ground versus a relatively small urn of ashes buried in a cemetery or cremation garden, inurned in a columbarium (a chamber or wall where urns are stored), kept at home (keep the cats away!), or scattered on land or sea. We're planning on being turned into ashes of some sort and have given much thought as to where we would like our ashes dispersed, since they won't stay in an urn for long. Actually, it can be quite fun and creative to think of new ways to throw your self (also known as cremains) to the wind.

A crematorium in Manchester, England, has introduced the idea of using heat produced by burning bodies to warm the people who come to mourn. Heat generated from the cremation process can produce enough power to run the boiler and light the chapel. The idea has already been given the green light by locals. Rev. Dr. Vernon Marshall of Old Chapel called it a "final act of generosity that is a lovely way for the dead to provide comfort for the living at a difficult time."

Cremating bodies in North America is one thing, but in India, where the population is approximately 800 million and the Hindu religion dictates that bodies are burned and not buried—using wood, no less—it takes a lot of trees to incinerate the number of people who die each year. The *Los Angeles Times* has reported that "devout Hindus regard cremation as an essential rite that frees the soul from the body, enabling its journey to the next level" and that "the demand for funeral pyres strips the country of more than 50 million trees annually, according to some estimates." The challenge of cremating or disposing of millions of people is obviously a world issue, and because of that, scientists, engineers, and regular citizens are focusing on innovative solutions to the problem.

DO YOU WANT TO BE CREMATED?

DO YOU WANT TO BE IN A COFFIN DURING CREMATION?

_____

_____

WHAT, IF ANYTHING, DO YOU WANT TO WEAR FOR YOUR CREMATION?

_____

_____

Do you wish to have your family there for a service or to witness the placing of the body in the cremation chamber? In most situations the cremation providers will permit family members to be in attendance when the body is placed into the cremation chamber. A few religious groups actually include this as part of their funeral practice.

In some states you are required to buy a coffin to be cremated in, which we think is crazy. It's a waste of wood and the extra fuel it takes to burn more materials. Plus, if the wood is particleboard, poisons are emitted into the atmosphere from the glue. Check your state laws, because sometimes you may be given the wrong impression by a salesperson. We recommend a cardboard coffin whenever possible, no matter what funeral directors try to talk you into.

In Siam, the ceremony of cremating the king was an elaborate ritual. The body was seated, mercury poured down the throat to dry it out, and fluids were captured for a state ceremony each day. When dried, the body was placed in an urn for about a year. Elaborate preparations then took place—the building of a 300-foot pyre of sandalwood and seven days of public games. The king was finally burned, and later the ashes were mixed with clay and given out to the people as souvenirs.

Another question you may have is whether you need to have the body embalmed before cremation. Unless you are having a viewing, it is actually against the law for a funeral home to tell you it is required. And don't worry, keep your pants on—later on, we'll talk about what kind of urn you want and where you want your ashes dispersed. You don't want to miss that part!

PROMESSION

What do an organic gardener, pink powder, and a bottle of Italian wine have to do with corpses? Sounds like the beginning of a joke, doesn't it? Well, a Swedish biologist, organic gardener, and wine drinker, Susanne Wiigh-Masak (our kind of gal!) invented a technique that essentially freezes the body and reduces it to an environmentally safe pink powder. Susanne got the name for it from a bottle of Italian wine called Promessa, which means promise. As a biologist and gardener, she was interested in the composting process. She asked the meat industry how they disposed of waste, and that led her to investigate freeze-drying by using liquid nitrogen, which is easily available as a by-product of oxygen bottling for medical use.

In a nutshell, the body is freeze-dried in liquid nitrogen, which makes it very brittle. Then the corpse is placed into a vibrating container, called a promator, which shatters it into powder by ultrasonic vibration, leaving a pile of nutritious pink powder. The remains are placed in a biodegradable coffin made of potato or cornstarch, which is put in a small grave under just eight inches of topsoil and composted by worms and bugs within six months to a year. In 2006, interest in promession seemed quite high. As of this writing, the Swedish authorities have finally given the go-ahead to sell promators. South Korea has already purchased 100 units.

RESOMATION

"Boiling the body . . . it is not!"
—*Sandy Sullivan, founder of Resomation, Ltd.*

Okay, Sandy, don't get excited. We understand. You claim that it is a chemical hydrolysis (with added alkali) at high temperature (170° C) with the body immersed in water. Boiling is a phase change where water is turned to steam. This system, however, is under high pressure, and boiling does not happen. The body tissues are transformed in thirty minutes into liquid and back to their original organic building blocks. What comes from all of this is a fine white powder and some liquids. Any dental fillings and metal body parts (artificial joints, pacemakers, etc.) are extracted and discarded.

But it still sounds like boiling. (Don't get mad at us!) It might take people a while to get used to this new process—not unlike when cremation was introduced and people couldn't get used to the idea of "burning Mother."

We were disappointed to find out that only about a thousand bodies have been processed with resomation. Coming out as a fine white powder intrigues us. Our imaginations started working overtime about screenplays where drug dealers pretend to be "resomation specialists" and distribute the powder as the ashes of a deceased person, only to find out that the white stuff being transported is actually . . . cocaine! Of course it would be easy to murder people and totally get away with it this way, since there is no DNA value and as a result, no connection to the original owner. (Maybe we'll pitch a show to HBO.) The process is environmentally friendly (no mercury or gas emissions, no chemicals released into the soil), the cost is low (approximately $600), the liquid can be used as fertilizer, and we like the idea of a beautiful white powder. (Don't call it "blow"!)

This all sounds good to us, and based on our research, we hope this process becomes accessible to the general public soon. This is our choice for now as we expect that there will be a resomation explosion (forgive us) before we die.

IF AND WHEN PROMESSION AND RESOMATION BECOME AVAILABLE
TO THE PUBLIC IN THE UNITED STATES, WOULD YOU PREFER EITHER
PROCESS? WHICH ONE? WHY?

_____

_____

As the percentage of cremations in the United States rises, so does the number of abandoned urns. Nationwide, more than thirty thousand cremation ash packages sit unclaimed on mortuary shelves.

SWEEPING UP THE ASHES

(Keep your hands out of the cookie jar!)

What to do with the cremains or ashes can be daunting after a loved one dies. And a reminder—if promession and resomation become available, you will have at least some powder left over, so you're not off the hook here, either. If you've made plans already for your remains, good for you. If not, you might want to take your time and let ideas come to you. After all, you may be spending a lot of time in that container. Most crematoriums will send you home with a plastic bag of ashes in a cardboard box, and the ashes will be perfectly fine in that until you're ready to move forward.

The great thing about ashes is that they're so portable, plus they can be divvied up and dispensed any way you and your loved ones wish. All you need are those little snack-size plastic bags. Little bags of your ashes will fit in purse or pocket, wallet, golf bag, glove compartment, eyeglass case, whatever. Your loved ones can keep taking you to all the places you loved in life!

Although most Japanese funeral services are held in the Buddhist traditional style, there is some variation. One custom takes place on the day the body is cremated. The guests take a meal in the crematorium. Afterwards, the relatives pick the bones out of the ash and pass them from person to person by chopsticks and place them into an urn.

The Internet is a gold mine for any kind of cremation urn or death memorabilia you can imagine and some you can't. A recent Google search for "Cremation Urns" came up with 608,000 hits. "Urns" produced 3,600,000 hits. How are you going to cull through all these websites? We're going to help. The key is to pick and choose your defining words carefully. Once you find a site you like,

A national study by the Funeral and Memorial Information Council released in 2007 found more Americans are now choosing cremation over burials—46 percent, up from 39 percent in 1995. Of those who preferred cremation, only about half wanted their remains kept in an urn, the study found. The rest wanted their ashes scattered over some favorite place, left in a cemetery, or brought home. Tellingly, about 14 percent had no idea what they wanted done with their remains.

you can surf through all the containers for the right one for you.

Narrowing your search can keep you from losing your mind while you're doing your research. One word of advice—when you find a site you like, check and see if they are members of the Better Business Bureau Online, the International Cemetery and Funeral Association (ICFA), the National Funeral Directors Association (NFDA), or any reputable association that polices online establishments. Not all online stores have to be associated with these sites, but take the time to scrutinize. Unfortunately, as we mentioned before, there are some unscrupulous people out there who are all too happy to take advantage of grieving individuals—this also applies in the cyberworld. That's another great reason to plan ahead!

Perhaps you have a hobby, a favorite sport, or secret wish you've been hiding. We're going to take you on a short tour of some creative cremation urns and containers, which should give you some sense of the possibilities that are out there:

❋ A custom-made (read: expensive) 31" x 7" Cigar Cremation Urn that can be used as a humidor (humidity activation charger is included) until "needed." Check it out at www.perfectmemorials.com/grande-esplendido-cigar-cremation-urn

❋ Handmade Bone Inlay Cremation Urn—gorgeous handmade wooden boxes with bone inlay. We want to go ahead and buy them now, and if we don't give them away as housewarming gifts before we die, we'll have (part of) our remains rest in them. www.funeral-urn.com

❋ Major League Baseball Urns are available in team themes: Atlanta Braves, Baltimore Orioles, Boston Red Sox, Chicago Cubs, Chicago White Sox, Cleveland Indians, Detroit Tigers, Los Angeles Dodgers, New York Mets, New York Yankees, Philadelphia Phillies, San Francisco Giants, and St. Louis Cardinals. Full-size caskets also come in sports team themes.www.eternalimage.net

❖ Huggable Urns—these snuggly teddy bears have a zippered pouch to hold cremains. The survivors can hug their loved ones whenever they want. www. huggableurns.com

❖ Star Trek Urn—features the twenty-fourth century styling of the United Federation of Planets and Starfleet. www.eternalimage.net

❖ Vintage McCoy Touring Car Cookie Jar— eBay has hundreds of vintage cookie jars on sale all the time, and most of them are usually way under $100. Try finding one that fits you—are you a "wise old owl" or are you feeling more like an "old raggedy Andy" about now? http://search.ebay.com/search

❖ Funeria—If you're interested in a buying a unique urn or vessel or commissioning a one-of-a-kind piece, this company works with some great artists. We especially loved the beautifully sculpted dog head. www.funeria.com

❖ Vatican Library Collection Urns—At last! The Vatican Library Collection endorses the products, and a percentage of the proceeds benefit the work of the Vatican Library Collection. "The urns are works of art. When people see them they usually give a little gasp—they are visually so stunning."

Also stunning is the array of different urns on the countless websites. There is an urn for almost every personality. Here's a brief peek: fly fishing urns, book urns, butterfly urns, lighthouse urns, sitting doves urns, golf bag urns, clock urns (tick-tock, time is up!), urns covered in dozens of porcelain roses, personal message box urns, Asian headrest urns, cowboy boot urns, two-person urns, motorcycle tank urns, pyramid urns, scuba diver urns, and Michelangelo's Pietà urns (no copyright issues, we presume).

In 1886, the Roman Catholic Church officially banned cremation. As recently as World War II, church members were excommunicated for arranging cremation.

WHAT KIND OF URN WOULD YOU LIKE? IF YOU HAVE A SPECIFIC ONE, PUT DOWN THE INFORMATION NEEDED TO BUY IT OR AT LEAST A VERY GOOD DESCRIPTION. (YOU MAY WANT TO BUY ONE IN ADVANCE TO BE SURE YOU HAVE THE PERFECT ONE FOR YOU.)

_____

_____

_____

_____

You might find that over the years your chosen urn doesn't work for you anymore (for example, if you selected one that looks like a hooker and you subsequently get married to a devout Christian, then you might want to think about changing that urn to say, a big cross.) On the other hand, don't be shamed into selecting one that isn't you—go for the golf clubs if you feel like it!

MORE THOUGHTS ON BODY DONATION AND CREMATION:

_____

_____

_____

_____

_____

_____

_____

_____

_____

_____

_____

_____

_____

_____

_____

_____

_____

_____

_____

_____

_____

_____

_____

_____

_____

_____

_____

_____

_____

_____

_____

_____

_____

_____

_____

_____

CHAPTER 7

FREEZE, ❋ BOIL, ❋ LIQUEFY, ❋ AND ❋ PRESERVE:

OTHER "RECIPES" FOR THE REMAINS

Y ou ain't heard nothin' yet! As we researched what to do with the remains, we found that people are even more un-usual than you could have ever imagined. And we know unusual.

CRYONICS:
Out of the Fire into the Freezer

Cryonics is the practice of deep-freezing human bodies at the moment of death for preservation and possible revival in the future. Those in the business of cryonics consider death to be a neurological process that begins after the heart stops. A stopped heart only causes death if nothing is done, so there must be some brain activity in order for the body to be preserved. Ideally, the cryonics cooling procedures should begin within the first minute or two after, and prefer-ably within fifteen minutes of heart cessation. This is why you need to have a contract with a cryonics company in advance—so that their technicians will be with you as you die or immediately afterwards. Time is definitely of the essence in this situation. Be aware that in the United States the freezing process can only be performed on people who are declared legally dead.

The most famous person who has ever been preserved using cryonics is baseball legend Ted Williams. Since his death in 2002, his body has been stored in a ten-foot stainless steel container. His head is in a smaller canister in Arizona. In 2004 a New York art gallery kicked off their season with the world premiere of an exhibition titled "The Ted Williams Memorial Display with Death Mask." The centerpiece of the show was the unveiling of the death mask of Williams's clinically decapitated frozen head.

Once the body arrives at a cryonics facility, it is cooled in liquid nitrogen to minus 200 degrees Fahrenheit—a temperature that stops physical decay. From that moment on, you'll be called a cryopreserved person, not a corpse, because the industry doesn't consider you to be dead. Be aware that cryonics cannot work for anyone who is truly brain dead. (If you thought we're going to make a blonde joke here—you're wrong!)

You're going to need some money (or a really good life insurance policy, which a cryonics company will help you set up) if you want to see what your future will look like. Without a body it will be pretty limited. You'll have to have a friend who is willing to carry your head around, maybe on their shoulder. Nagging not allowed. Anyway, we've seen prices range from $28,000 to $80,000 for head-only cryopreservation to $150,000 for the whole body. If you're really interested, we suggest you get in touch with one of the companies and have them go through their various memberships. (It sounds a bit like a health club—let's hope not the kind where you pay and never show up.)

It's alive! Researchers at the University of Minnesota have created a beating rat heart in a laboratory. The researchers removed all the cells from a dead rat heart, leaving the valves and outer structure as framework for new heart cells from newborn rats. Within two weeks the new cells formed a new beating heart that conducted electrical impulses and pumped a small amount of blood. Does this mean we won't have to go to the gym anymore?

There is now an experimental method of freezing organs in cryobiology called vitrification. It is the process, still under development, of converting a material such as organs into a glasslike amorphous solid that is free from any crystalline structure. It's like what happens when lightning hits sand and glass is made, except it's gooey. It's also like a cellular form of antifreeze, so that tissues and organs can be exposed to supercold temperatures without worrying about damaging ice crystals forming. Research shows that suspended animation of an organ begins somewhere around minus 180 degrees Fahrenheit. Then the organ is left in a cryopreservative substance that keeps it vital for future use. As of this writing, vitrification is not yet a viable process for things other than semen, blood, eggs, and embryos, although it is now widely regarded as the most promising approach for long-term banking of large organs. They can now cool a rabbit kidney to minus 7 degrees for about one hour, rewarm it, and transplant it as a working kidney. But the temperature is not cold enough to achieve vitrification. We hope this process revolutionizes organ donor programs in the near future.

We have to admit that we were skeptical about this cryonics thing at first, but the more we found out about it, the more we love (some things) about it! Cryopreservation is used in infertility programs. Think about it: lots and lots of those frozen tissues are sperm and human eggs and embryos just waiting to thaw out and end up as bundles of joy. Talk about bursts of huge love and energy all over the world!

Tardigrades, also known as water bears, are microscopic animals that can survive under severe conditions for centuries. They can endure minus 273 degrees Centigrade, tolerate dry and high heat conditions to 150 degrees Celsius, and even survive in a vacuum. They have helped scientists to find practical implications for medicine and freezing human tissue for space study, as well as how to survive in extreme conditions.

There is a high representation of scientists among cryonics advocates. Scientific support for cryonics is based on studies showing substantial preservation of brain cell structure by current methods, and projections of future technology, especially molecular nanotechnology and nanomedicine. Some scientists believe that future medicine will enable molecular-level repair and regeneration of damaged tissues and organs decades or centuries in the future. Disease and aging are also assumed to be reversible. It should be no surprise that many ethical questions revolve around the issue of whether cryonics can or should work.

PLASTINATION:
A New Definition of Hard-Body

A more controversial method of preserving the body has been used to create one of the most popular museum exhibits ever, inspiring many people to donate their bodies for permanent display. Nearly 25 million people worldwide have seen skinned bodies perfectly preserved and displayed through a process described as "forced vacuum impregnation" by its inventor Dr. Gunther von Hagens of Heidelberg, Germany. The multimillionaire doctor discovered plastination in 1977 and staged the first public exhibition of his work in 1987. He is a former anatomy professor who believes the knowledge gained from plastinated bodies is invaluable.

Plastinated humans are dissected to demonstrate the workings of the body, even showing clear examples of the nervous system and the circulatory system. Most appear to be stripped of their skin in order to expose the body's musculature. Since starting the traveling exhibits, Dr. von Hagens has shown a plastinated hurdler in mid-jump, one riding a bike, another dribbling a basketball, a horse and rider split into two parts and a pregnant woman with her torso open to reveal the fetus. In response to the controversy of using real human bodies, Dr. von Hagens says, "Nothing can match the real thing. Why not look into a book of nice trees instead of going into the woods? You will feel more apprehension and tension upon seeing real bodies, and strong emotions will make your memory last longer and allow you to retain the information better." He has plans for creating a plastination zoo that will include a camel, gorilla, giraffe, and even an elephant.

The plastination process involves replacing the normal liquid found in human tissue and cells with clear liquid plastic polymer through the use of acetone and vacuum impregnation—in effect turning human tissue into plastic. Dissection and plastination of an entire body requires about 1,500 working hours and normally takes about one year to complete. Bodies and body parts that have been recently plastinated are still soft and pliable and may be put into a multitude of positions. Then the plastinates are cured by heat and special gases to harden them into permanent poses.

Many people regard Dr. von Hagens's work as art. Some universities prefer to use the plastinates for instruction instead of traditional cadaver dissection. Dr. von Hagens uses only voluntarily donated bodies and never uses unclaimed corpses. As of June 2007, approximately 8,000 people from around the world have entered their names on the body donor register for the Plastinarium. Dr. von Hagens's "collaboration with donors" includes his best friend, who willed his body for dissection and display. The doctor and his wife will also be plastinated after their deaths.

Ironically, Dr. von Hagens's native Germany has not been so receptive to his displays of truly "naked" bodies. He says that, "In Germany there's a historic reason because of our German Nazi past . . . it always creates a kind of remembrance of corpses in concentration camps." England has also been resistant to Body Worlds exhibitions because it reminds people of the time when cadavers of executed criminals were made available for public autopsies.

Even so, Dr. von Hagens says donors who choose plastination for eternity "can express their wishes—what kind of pose, what kind of specimen they are going to be transformed into after death. They are better off than even the mummies of the pharaohs." As one donor wrote in the donor register, "No rotting in the ground for me or quick release as a puff of smoke from some crematorium chimney. I wanted to be here with the other exhibits—skinned, posed, and proud."

So, is plastination something you're interested in? Just think . . . your corpse could be around forever for everyone to see and admire, and you can make it tap dance or kick a football or pose in any way you wish.

MUMMIFICATION:
From Here to Eternity

The term *mummy* comes from the Arabic word *mummiya*, which refers to bitumen—a black, sticky component of tar used by the ancient Egyptians in embalming. If you're like us, you've been fascinated with ancient Egypt since you were a kid, and what could be more intriguing and scary than mummies? Until we began writing this book, we didn't know that we could end up as one.

Have you secretly harbored a wish to be like Cleopatra, Queen Nefertiti, or Ramses II? Summum—an official religious and tax-exempt organization based in Salt Lake City—offers everything you need to make those dreams of mummification come true. Summum was founded in 1975 by Claude Rex Nowell, who legally changed his name to Summum Bonum Amon Ra—but goes by the name of "Corky" Ra. Summum works with funeral companies around the country. After your death, your body will be taken to your local funeral home, where it will be prepared for the traditional viewing and funeral services. Afterwards you'll be transported to Salt Lake City to begin the mummification rites. The mummification process is a unique, patented procedure that takes between three and four months. At the end of it all, you'll weigh one or two tons—with the sarcophagus. We aren't particularly thrilled with those numbers, but we've never seen a fat mummy, so we're not going to worry about it.

Mummification is not cheap. A $67,000

And you thought your teacher was boring. Jeremy Bentham (1748–1831), the founder of Utilitarianism, had his body embalmed, mounted in a glass case, and put on permanent display at University College, London. It remains there to this day and apparently is still wheeled in to preside over the annual meeting of university administrators.

"donation" will cover the cost of being embalmed. Another $100,000-plus will get you a bronze or stainless steel "mummiform" with inlaid gold, ceramics, or jewels, if that's what you want. Over 14,500 people have paid in advance or bought life insurance policies (some worth over $350,000) so they can be mummified and placed in special sanctuaries of their choosing. Mohamed al-Fayed, the father of Princess Diana's boyfriend Dodi, has signed on and built a sphinx with his face on it. It's on display at Harrods Department Store in London.

According to Ron Permu at Summum, the organization receives about 300 Internet inquiries for downloads of their legal documents every day. After Walt Disney's wife refused to honor his cryogenic contract and cremated him instead, Corky had all legal documents necessary for mummification placed on the Internet, so that immediate family, children, lawyers, and executors of estates could sign them. Summum will not mummify anyone

Scattered throughout northern Japan are two dozen self-mummified monks who were followers of Shugendo, an ancient form of Buddhism. For three years a priest would eat only nuts and seeds while doing rigorous physical activity that reduced all his body fat. For the next three years he ate only bark and roots. Afterward, he began drinking a poisonous tea made from a sap containing Urushiol (the same thing that makes poison ivy), which caused vomiting and a rapid loss of body fluids. Finally, he would sit in the lotus position and lock himself in a stone tomb. Each day he rang a bell. When the bell stopped ringing, the tomb was sealed.

who does not have written permission from every family member and legal advisor.

Only some small Buddhist sects and Summum are making mummies today. According to Corky Ra, "The ancient Egyptians turned people into a dried object like beef jerky. Our wet process keeps the body fresh and supple." We like the company's approach to health clubs: "Why spend thousands of dollars in health club fees while you're alive," said Ra, "and then let everything go to pot just because you've died?"

As of this writing there have not yet been any human mummifications, but Summum has done lots and lots of successful and endearing pet mummifications. The company has an informative and entertaining website that the whole family can enjoy. Check it out at www.summum.org/mummification.

So let's just say you've decided to cremate your body (after you've donated your organs and tissues) because you can't yet put it through the processes of promession or resomation in the United States. You could mummify it, but the costs are extraordinarily high, so that's a deterrent. And the plastination people are in Germany and China, and they may already have enough corpses for their expensive traveling show, so that's another deterrent. But your family has a nice pile of ashes to do something with, and you would like them to try something different. Let's assume your relatives agree and will go along with your wishes. Here are some fabulous options.

BURIAL AT SEA:
One Last Splash

This is not new, but it's quickly becoming more popular. Many companies have sprung up in the past few years, making it quite easy to throw your ashes in a variety of watery locales. You can even ship your ashes to companies all over the world that will do it for your family, if they can't make it or they're prone to seasickness.

We're huge fans of the ocean, and we may disperse some of our ashes there—most likely in the Atlantic—either off the coast of Maine or off New York harbor or both. Dream dispersals include off the shores of Capri or Sicily and into the Aegean Sea from the Temple of Poseidon at Cape Sounion. We like to make people work hard to please us. Frankly, we love the symbolism of going back to where our ancestors crawled out to create new life (of course this was around 6,000 years ago). Think about sea dispersal if you love the water. Of course lakes and rivers are an option too, if you choose carefully or your family moves fast enough when it's not legally allowed.

A sampling of people whose ashes were buried at sea:

Adolf Eichmann
Ingrid Bergman
Janis Joplin
Jerry Garcia
John F. Kennedy, Jr.
L. Ron Hubbard
Robert Heinlein
Robert Mitchum
Rock Hudson
Steve McQueen
Vincent Price

ETERNAL REEFS:
It's Not Just Cement Shoes

Here is an inspired, fairly new way of dispersing ashes. It's another kind of green burial that helps save coral reefs, so many of which have been decimated in the recent past. Eternal Reefs has designed a way of restoring our coastlines using a patented design for cement "reef balls," and now they have given you the opportunity of choosing to be a part of that healing process by mixing your ashes into a memorial reef. These are large cement balls with holes in them, allowing water to flow through, thus preventing them from rolling around when placed on the ocean floor, even during major storms.

When a family wishes to memorialize a loved one (you perhaps), they will participate in casting one of these reef balls, with the deceased's ashes folded into the cement mixture. Inscriptions may be marked in the wet cement along with a permanent plaque displaying the deceased's name, dates, and possibly a personal message. It is customary to takes rubbings from these plaques for family keepsakes. The funeral is a separate event from the memorial ceremony at the casting of the reef ball. And if you qualify, military honors, including the playing of "Taps" and the presenting of a flag, may be combined with a memorial reef viewing. Your family can even get a mini-memorial reef ball for mantle or desktop, along with pendants that have your name and coordinates inscribed on the back.

Frequently a pet's remains have been mixed with their human companions into reef balls. Of course you can do a separate reef ball for your pet, called the "Pearl" memorial reef. And you can almost get two for the price of one by mixing a second person's remains into your eternal reef for a nominal fee—perfect for longtime couples, groupings of family members, or boss and employee (just kidding!).

Reef balls also help to restore much-needed marine habitats. A few years after Eternal Reefs has situated your ball in one of the many permitted ocean locations, living overgrowth will cover the memorial reef. Swimming with the fishes for eternity can be a wonderful statement about your love of the environment and your sincere desire to help Mother Earth. We are seriously considering this option, but of course we do this with almost every way of disposing of the body. We can't help it if we like them all so much; we're like the Willard Scott of funeral planning—everything is our favorite!

There is something brand new in the ash disposal business—the world's first underwater columbarium—also known as The Neptune Memorial Reef. It is a sixteen-acre piece of until-this-time barren area of white sand, fifty feet under water, just three and a quarter miles off the Miami coast. It is designed to look like the lost city of Atlantis (aged a bit), using 2,000 tons of environmentally safe cement. There is also a set of twelve-foot entrance gates guarded by a pair of bronze lions.

Eventually this underwater undertaker's paradise will be able to hold the cremated remains of 125,000 people, each one mixed with a bit of cement and inserted into openings placed throughout the structure. The creators spent years designing and getting the approval and coordination of nearly a dozen governmental agencies. They intended Neptune Memorial Reef to be a special place for memorializing people who love the sea and to serve as an undersea breakwater to help reduce erosion of the ocean's floor as well as a large and active marine research site.

In the United States, ashes must be scattered at least three miles from shore, and bodies may be given to the sea if the location is at least 600 feet deep. Each religion has its own specific procedures for burial at sea. For instance:

❧ ANGLICANISM – the ship must be stopped; the body must be sewn in sailcloth, together with two cannon balls for weight, and lowered into the sea.

❧ CATHOLICISM – the church is against scattering remains on ground, air, or sea. Burial at sea in a casket or urn is allowed if the deceased died at sea.

❧ LUTHERANISM – Many Lutheran naval veterans and seamen prefer to be buried at sea. The casket or urn is set to sea or ashes are scattered.

ASHES TO ASHES, DUST TO DIAMONDS:
Betty is Bling and so is Ben

Has anyone ever told you your eyes sparkle like diamonds? What if your eyes were made into diamonds—along with the rest of your body—or at least a few ounces of your cremated remains? In the new age of commemorating your loved ones, instead of giving a diamond to express your love, they can make you into one. It's a unique segment of the $25 billion death-care industry, which has been finding different ways of dealing with deceased persons' ashes, as more people opt to be cremated. This process has caught the imagination of people who want to become diamonds, as well as the people they left behind—those who desire an indestructible (almost), timeless memento of their loved ones. Unlike an urn of your ashes, which frequently ends up in the closet, this is something your family can have with them always.

These gems are created by essentially speeding up a process that normally takes millions of years in nature. Carbon is extracted from a small amount of your cremains, heated, converted to graphite, then put into a diamond press and exposed to tremendous heat and pressure. The diamonds created are identical in all properties to real

Memorial Glass, a Sonoma, California, company, has been making glass memorial products out of cremains for over a decade. Their products have included paperweights, pendants, and earrings. "We've made goblets, whatever people ask for," says Leslie Moody, cofounder of the company. So far, that's included bowls, heart-shaped keepsakes, and even "drinking glasses out of my husband's mother." (Mother-in-law's are so transparent.)

diamonds. Each person has enough carbon in them to create fifty to one hundred diamonds!

As you might imagine, a process like this does not come cheap. They range from a few thousand dollars up to almost $20,000 for a full-carat beauty. Sizes larger than 1 ½ carats can be made, but you need to contact Lifegem.com, the company that patented the process. The variety is impressive—you can choose different colors, sizes, cuts, and settings. You can even have your pet formed into dazzling rings, lockets, or earrings. Me-ow!

When you think about it, it's not unlike the Victorians, who put pieces of the deceased's hair in lockets. Some people may think this is morbid, but we rather like the idea. Maybe you'd like to make some diamonds out of your deceased husband or your pet dog. It gives a whole new meaning to the term *family jewels*. Are you thinking you'd like to be hanging on your wife's neck or carried around on your daughter's middle finger? We thought that might be the case. By the way, there is also a company that makes a more economical zircon out of your pet's ashes. A handcrafted cut and polished Pet-Gem starts at only $275 through Pet-Gems.com.

VARIETY IS THE SPICE OF DEATH!

Of course there are even more options if your loved ones want to carry your ashes with them at all times. There is a proliferation of jewelry pieces—essentially containers for bits of ash—such as a heart locket, a crystal pendant, an art glass pendant swirling with ashes, and dozens of other shapes in gold or silver, including cylinders, crosses, turtles, butterflies, cowboy boots, hands in prayer, dog bones, sunflowers, shells, roses, a child's portrait, teardrops, minimal geometric shapes, and hearts with a photo imprinted. We suggest you choose a particular piece that you feel connected to in advance and have several of them given out as gifts at your funeral—just like bridesmaids' gifts given out at weddings!

UPS and FedEx will not accept cremated remains for shipment. Cremated remains may be shipped through the U.S. Postal Service, but they must be shipped by registered mail with return receipt requested. Be sure to double-box the container, with adequate stuffing between the two boxes to prevent any damage. Make sure the person on the receiving end is expecting the package and can travel to the post office to sign for it.

THE CREMAINING OPTIONS

Paint by Embers...
After They've Cooled

There is a way they won't be able to forget you, even if they want to—have a portrait painted of you using paint mixed with your cremains! Do a bit of searching on this one if you like the idea—there are different artists with varying degrees of expertise and style. You may even want an abstract painting where the painter tries to channel your energy as they paint (no joke). We suggest if you know any artists or know of an artist whose work you admire, ask them if they would try painting with some of your ashes—even if it is the first time they've done this. It just adds a bit of texture to the paint, which can be interesting. This area is in its nascent stages, so we're sure the quality and variety of the paintings will improve. If it works, it's a wonderful way to be remembered—you've always been a work of art, anyway!

Pencils (Don't Chew on These!)

If you're a writer or great note taker, or you're constantly bugging your kids to do their homework—you may like your ashes to be made into pencils. This is another great "bridesmaids/groomsmen/guests" gift for your funeral celebration. It certainly says something about your sharp wit!

Beam Me Up: The Living End

If it's good enough for Scotty, then it's something to consider. *Star Trek* creator Gene Roddenberry and actor James Doohan both chose a most appropriate way for their final sendoff—into outer space. They're circling Earth right now, happy to be in their favorite environment—the last frontier (after death, that is). Comet-spotter Eugene Shoemaker must have had connections, because he had his ashes buried on the Moon.

If you always wanted to be an astronaut or you love outer space and other worlds, then you can honor those feelings by circling the Earth or the Moon, or going out into deep space on Celestis Inc.'s Voyager Service. This deluxe service is expected to launch its first mission in 2009 aboard a spacecraft being developed that will utilize a solar sail for propulsion. Memorial Space Flights range from $495 for a trip out and back, to $67,495 for fourteen grams of two people's ashes launched on the Voyager Service. These prices include an invitation to the launch and memorial services, pre-launch briefings, launch tour (where available), a DVD of the launch, and a personal online memorial.

Up in a Balloon:
Letting Go of Dead Loved Ones

How many businesses do you know that start with a husband saying to his wife, "Just put my butt in a balloon and send me off"? That's how Eternal Ascent, a company that sends your cremation ashes up in a balloon, came into being. The couple already owned a bridal shop and had the equipment on hand, so they sent their beloved cat's ashes up in one of their five-foot biodegradable balloons—which eventually led to the husband's comment.

People have been sending family members' ashes up in their giant helium balloons ever since. If you're still a kid at heart, a balloon release is both fun and elegant, and your ashes are released in the atmosphere, eventually wafting back to Earth. Cost is $1,600 for everything; a DVD of the ceremony is extra.

Mummified, stuffed, freeze-dried—who cares when it's your loved one? The price of having your pet stuffed and mounted starts at around $2,000. The most famous example is Roy Rogers's horse, Trigger. At Anthony Eddy's Wildlife Studio in Missouri, you can have your pet freeze-dried, and the result is similar to having the pet mounted. The process involves freezing and the use of a vacuum. It can take up to nine months for a small cat and eighteen months to two years for a large dog. The larger animals cost from $700 to about $5,000. "Turkey heads are our bread and butter, but we do about 100 pets a year—iguanas, snakes, cockatiels, baby kittens, dogs," said Mac Krog, who works at AEWS.

Fireworks:
They'll Have Stars in Their Eyes!

Fireworks are perhaps the most celebratory way of making a blowout statement about who you are and how you feel about life. We love the idea of our cremains shooting out in a blaze of glory. It's a bit expensive (at Angels Flight Inc. it ranges from $3,750 to $4,900), but it's one of our very favorites for lifting the spirits of your grieving family and friends. Actually, compared to the average cost of a funeral, it's not a bad deal and much more fun. Who can be sad when they see fireworks? This kind of sendoff expresses so much: Life was a blast and I loved it! Whoopee! I'm free! I want to fill you with joy and wonder as a last gift. Celebrate me and don't mourn too long because I'm doing great! I'm off to heaven! I was so very, very happy to have been here on Earth with you, I'm kissing the sky in gratitude.

The great writer Hunter Thompson enjoyed numerous hallucinogenic fantasies in his life but none better than the fabulous funeral his friend Johnny Depp threw for him when he died. Some of the 350 guests included George McGovern, Lyle Lovett, Senator John Kerry, and Ed Bradley. Thompson's ashes were blown into the sky over his farm, carried by red, blue, and silver fireworks. It all took place in front of a giant 153-foot dagger monument, topped with a doubled-thumbed gonzo fist that Mr. Thompson had designed thirty years before. The statue was two feet taller than the Statue of Liberty. At a price of two million dollars, a good time was had by all.

What would Carmen do?

Carmen has inclinations, if her husband Vern goes before her, to put his ashes to good use. She sees it as a permanent visitation from him at all moments. First she would take some ashes and form them into a little "coral reef" for a home aquarium. Then she'd paint a picture of him in his favorite color with a cremains/paint mix and most probably he would be laughing or blowing her an air kiss. After that, she'd build a cremation-ash birdhouse for the orioles and chickadees, because birds can symbolize eternity and love. Each spring there would be new life, in the form of chicks, peeping over Vern. Don't think of the bird guano—focus on the positive.

She would then mix a bit of ashes into some clay at one of those "make-it-yourself" pottery shops, creating plates decorated with Vern's likeness and his favorite sayings, like, "Oh, brother!" and "Do you love me, Honey?" Continuing in that mode, she'd fashion a mug with the saying, "You're not forgettin' me, are you, honey?" painted on the bottom, so she would see it as she drank her last drop of coffee in the morning.

Of course, being a gardener, she would replenish the soil of her houseplants with Vern fertilizer and throw some over the vegetable garden, making her think of him as she ate the squash and tomatoes in a lovely stew. If she could find a glass blower artist, she would make a beautiful vase swirling with Vern's ashes to hold the flowers she'd grown with his rich ash fertilizer.

Being the practical type, Carmen might put some ashes into those door snakes (draft-stoppers), which are essentially cloth tubes filled with sand and placed along the insides of doors to keep the cold out. This is a new definition of your beloved warming your heart. "Vern Candles," made by adding his ashes and his favorite aftershave to the beeswax, would represent how he was the light of her life, not to get too corny or anything.

The body—you can bury it, donate it, burn it, liquefy it, freeze it, freeze-dry it, make it plastic, and mummify it. The variety of ways to deal with your body continues to amaze us. And we don't amaze easily. So be inspired as you expire and give 'em something to work with!

Bone China is a hybrid porcelain that contains six parts bone ash, four parts china stone, and three and a half parts of china clay. Bone china is easier to manufacture, is strong, does not chip easily and has an ivory-white appearance. There are some people that get a little queasy about eating off of real bone, so you might want to keep this information to yourself.

YOUR THOUGHTS ON FREEZING, BOILING, LIQUIFYING, AND PRESERVING:

_____

_____

_____

_____

_____

_____

_____

_____

_____

_____

_____

_____

_____

_____

_____

_____

_____

_____

_____

_____

_____

_____

_____

_____

_____

_____

_____

_____

CHAPTER 8

GRAVESIDE SERVICES

LOCATION, LOCATION, LOCATION

S ome people opt for just a graveside service instead of a full-blown funeral. This is referred to as "direct burial" by the funeral industry. You can certainly save some money doing just a graveside service. Plus, it can be more intimate, with a few family and friends. However, all the elements of a formal funeral may be included in this format: a pastor, priest, or speaker to conduct the service, music, flowers, "testimonials" by friends and family members, chairs, and personal touches such as photo boards. You may even want to have a portable bar just off to the side of the service—think of the graveside service as your last tailgating party.

There are as many options for graveside services as there are options for what to do with the body and ashes. In the next few pages you'll find all the basic elements for any service, so apply them to any type of service you choose. Perhaps fashion is your religion. Why not have everyone dress in your favorite color to celebrate you? If you are a diehard (get it?) Red Sox fan, have everyone wear the team colors. Maybe you're a member of the Red Hats club—go for it and try to get them to wear red hats. We think it's a good idea to embarrass people at your graveside service. It reminds them they're human.

Queen Victoria made a list of keepsakes she wanted to take with her to her grave. They included one of Prince Albert's dressing gowns, a plaster cast of his hand, numerous photographs, and several articles of jewelry. She also instructed that a lock of hair and a photograph of her devoted attendant and friend, John Brown, be placed in her left hand. The items were hidden from view in her casket by a cushion and a posy of flowers.

In ancient Rome, the poor were buried at night by torchlight. But well-to-do Romans hired professional undertakers, whose staff included funeral criers, musicians, singers of dirges, jesters, actors, and torchbearers, all of whom made a grand procession.

Who would you like to conduct your graveside ceremony? This should probably be someone who likes you. Or perhaps choose someone who has wronged you and feels very guilty about it. This is their chance to make it up to you and say all those wonderful things you always thought about yourself but were too embarrassed to say and for some reason no one else was saying, either. It's a good idea to "make suggestions" (dictate) here, if you can— just to help them out, of course.

It's perfectly okay to write your own service . . . who knows you better than you? Today, so many people write their own vows for their weddings, why not write your own eulogy and/or obituary? Tell yourself how much you love you and how you will always love you, till death did you part. We would like to see this become a new tradition! It's probably a good idea, however, to choose someone other than yourself to read the actual words.

Perhaps you would like everyone to sing a song—badly, which can be a great ice-breaker or a nice, sentimental touch. To view an example of a funny and moving song sung at an actual service, go to YouTube and find the Monty Python clan singing "Always Look on the Bright Side Life" at Graham Chapman's memorial service. The fact that this irreverent song is one of the most popular pieces of music requested at funerals gives us great faith in humanity. For any song you choose, have the words printed and passed out to the attendees, so no one has an excuse not to sing.

Until recently, in order to have music at the graveside, you had to hire musicians or singers for the event. Nowadays, with iPods and an array of MP3 players, you can have all the music you want wherever you want. As we've said, music is emotionally evocative and a wonderful way to convey your parting message. You might want to start putting your playlist together now, just in case—you know—you unexpectedly kick the bucket, buy the farm, push up daisies, take a dirt nap, go to meet your maker, go to a better place, check out, croak, rest in peace, whatever.

Think about how powerful the haunting sound of a single bugler playing "Taps" is while a soldier's body is lowered into the ground. Or bagpipes (one of our favorites) is especially moving (perhaps a version of "I Still Haven't Found What I'm Looking For" played on the pipes would be interesting). Think carefully about this decision—it will be the last time your loved ones will hear your "voice." Do you want to leave them laughing, crying, confused, resentful, amused, grief-stricken, or sobbing uncontrollably? The choice is yours (we prefer the last one).

Some people have had doves released while the body was being lowered into the ground. A word of caution: if your plot is next to a nature preserve with hawks flying around, you might want to rethink the doves. There was an unfortunate case of a dove being eaten mid-air after its release at a graveside service. In lieu of doves, try butterflies, balloons, or hornets and watch the fun from the other side!

Try having a champagne toast at your service, or have everyone shoot tequila, or throw glasses at the coffin like at Russian weddings—which is for good luck, a perfect sentiment in this case. Or you may want loved ones to throw herbs onto your coffin as it's being lowered. Many herbs have symbolic meanings: rosemary for remembrance, sorrel for affection, sage for esteem, and basil for love.

Finally, is there a parting song you want to play as people walk away from the service? This should be a signature song of yours; this is truly your last shot at saying something or creating a final mood. It's an incredibly poignant time, the air is already

The Zulus of Africa used to burn all the belongings of the deceased to prevent evil spirits from hovering in the vicinity. Some tribes would set up a ring of fire around dead bodies to singe the wings of the spirits and thus prevent them from attacking members of the community. Other tribes would throw spears and arrows into the air to kill any lingering spirits of the dead. They also believed that eating bitter herbs would drive away or kill the unwanted spirits.

filled with emotion, feeling, and sentiment. People are thinking of you and also of their own lives in ways they normally don't. You have a chance like no other to go deep into their hearts and minds. Think of the incredible setup—go ahead, hit them with your best shot!

After performances, certain singers have their own signature parting songs. For example, Bob Hope used to sing "Thanks for the Memories." We wonder if they played this at his funeral—think of the impact! Frank Sinatra had "My Way." (perfect!) Here are some more examples of parting graveside service songs—continue to keep the context in mind as you hum these in your head:

❖ Freddy Mercury, "We Are the Champions" (Well, you are, aren't you?)

❖ Etta James, "At Last" (Oh my God, perfectly heartbreaking here.)

❖ Martha Washington, "It's Raining Men" (Hallelujah! Great spirit.)

❖ Judy Garland, "Somewhere Over the Rainbow"
(Sobbing will ensue, almost no better song in this case.)

❖ Rick James, "Super Freak" (They will go out high and laughing! If you've lived a very prim and proper life, let your hair down and go out with this tune. You will shock them and they will never forget you.)

❖ Lena Horne, "Stormy Weather" (Very sad, tear-inducing.)

❖ Louis Prima, "Just a Gigolo" ("I ain't got nobody . . . "
Oddly, with that title, it's one of the most upbeat, joyous songs around.)

❖ Coolio, "Gangsta's Paradise" ("As I walk through the valley of death . . . ")

❖ U2, "Beautiful Day" ("It's a beautiful day . . . Don't let it get away.")

❖ David Bowie, "Changes" (Poignant and sexy. Wow!)

Now, let's get some thoughts, feelings, and ideas on your graveside service down on paper before we move on:

DO YOU WANT TO HAVE A GRAVESIDE SERVICE? IF SO, WHO DO YOU WANT TO ATTEND? (NO NEED TO LIMIT THE GUEST LIST BECAUSE YOU'RE NOT PAYING BY THE HEAD. THIS IS ONE ADVANTAGE TO A FUNERAL VERSUS A WEDDING—SO MUCH MORE ECONOMICAL!)

_____

_____

_____

_____

_____

_____

_____

_____

DO YOU WANT IT TO BE RELIGIOUS? IF SO, WHAT RELIGION?

_____

_____

WHO WOULD YOU LIKE TO CONDUCT THE SERVICE AND/OR READ PASSAGES AT THE SERVICE?

_____

_____

ARE THERE ANY SPECIFIC PASSAGES, POEMS, FAVORITE EXPRESSIONS, SONGS, PERSONAL STORIES, OR EVEN JOKES YOU'D LIKE TO INCLUDE?

_____

_____

DO YOU WANT MUSIC? IF SO, WHAT SONGS/PIECES?

_____

_____

IS THERE ANY SPECIAL MUSIC YOU'D LIKE TO HAVE PLAYING AS YOU'RE
LOWERED INTO YOUR B-SPOT?

_____

_____

ARE THERE ANY OTHER SPECIAL TOUCHES FOR YOUR GRAVESIDE
CEREMONY YOU WISH TO INCLUDE?

_____

_____

THE GREEN GRAVESIDE SERVICE:

It doesn't have to be boring and stiff

With some imagination, there are as many options for a green funeral graveside service as there are for conventional burial ceremonies. Since natural burials are relatively new in the United States, you are free to create new customs. It's a whole new world—well, what's old is new again. You can also get lots of ideas by going to British and Australian websites on green burial—they seem to be a bit ahead of us in this area. We believe the only real difference between traditional and green is what goes into the grave. You can do all sorts of graveside memorializing at both kinds of funerals.

We do have some ideas that might be particularly moving and soothing in this situation. If you've never heard a Tibetan singing bowl, go onto eBay and listen to a few of them. They each have different tonal qualities, so plan to spend some time to find one or a few that you like. Small ones may be given out as mementos, then all the attendants can ring them together and create music of you. Believe us, anyone attending will never forget this experience. This is not just for spiritual or so-called new age types—any one, any age, any sex , any religion can enjoy them. Think about drums, gongs, flutes, a mandolin, a cello, a violin—any instrument that travels well. We love the sound and the idea of a group of mourners doing a continuous "Omm" for a few minutes. This is a great group piece because everyone knows the

We called all the green cemeteries to see if drinking was allowed at the graveside services. They were fine with the concept. We believe they even agreed to a graveside bar with blenders for cosmos and complicated martinis. They have to be made of natural ingredients of course.

lyrics. Or bring an electric guitar (with an amplifier), lots of kazoos, maracas, or tambourines. You get the idea. If you were a third grade teacher, you can torture everyone with kazoos so they get a taste of what you went through in your life.

At burials, it's not uncommon for mourners to make a day of the event at a green graveside celebration. They spend hours digging, carrying the corpse to the grave, burying it, telling stories, singing songs, having a picnic, playing music, and reflecting the continuum of life . . . it goes on.

Here's a nondenominational "Celtic Prayer for The Newly Dead" that resonated with us and seems most appropriate for a ceremony in nature (we like the pagan aspect):

CELTIC PRAYER FOR THE NEWLY DEAD

May your journey to the Summerlands, the Isles of the Blessed,
to the heart of the Goddess, to the land of freedom and splendour,
be swift and sure.
You are blessed, you are blessed, you are blessed.
We ask that the blessing of the Spirits of the Tribe and of the Ancestors,
of Time and of Place and of the Journey be with you.
We ask that the blessing of the Spirits of North and South,
East and West be with you.
We ask that you might be blessed with fire and with water,
with earth and with air and with Spirit.
We ask for the blessing of the Lord and Lady of the Animals and the Woods,
the mountains and the streams,
And we ask that the blessing of the Uncreated One, of the Created Word,
and of the Spirit that is the Inspirer, be always with you.
By the beauty of the fields, the woods and the sea,
by the splendour that is set upon all that is,
we send you our love and blessings.
Go safely, go well, go surely. Our hearts are with you.
There is no separation.

BURIAL AT SEA:
Say Hello to Davy Jones

The first piece of advice we want to give you before you plan your burial at sea is to check out the boat. What could be worse than planning a beautiful sunset service on the ocean, and your family members find themselves bailing out water? Needless to say, burial at sea is irreversible, so make sure your family is in total agreement with such a burial beforehand.

Depending on the state, ashes may be scattered right off a dock or at least three miles from shore. A full-body burial has a whole different list of rules and regulations depending upon whether you're in a casket or not and whether it's a military funeral or a civilian one. There is one company that will replicate a full military burial-at-sea ceremony if you've had a less than honorable discharge, which we really appreciate, given human frailty and the challenges of today's world. If you choose an at-sea military funeral, it's done by the navy while they are on duty, so the family cannot attend.

If you're planning to scatter your ashes onto the sea, you might want to kill three birds with one boat trip—the graveside service, memorial service, and party. You can have anyone perform the ceremony, but many charter boat captains will do the honors. There are lots of ideas to memorialize you and leave people with a lasting memory and a memento. You need to set the tone for these events in advance. If you're interested in something more playful, nothing sets a

Carmen's father's requested to have some of his ashes spread over his parents' graves in North Carolina, with Carmen and Didi, her godmother, in attendance. While reciting the Lord's Prayer, they began to pour the ashes when a huge wind came out of nowhere and covered them with the cremains. At first they were stunned, and then they were overcome by fits of laughter. Carmen felt that her father, her grandparents, Didi, and she were all sharing a good laugh. Inadvertently it was the best graveside service she's ever attended.

celebratory atmosphere more than the sound of a champagne cork popping. We love the idea of casting out a wreath of your favorite flowers or a trail of rose petals as you go out to sea. If you're really adventurous, arrange to have snow globes made using memorial seawater, shells, cremains, and a picture of you on the bottom so that every time someone shakes it, they will see you winking at them.

DO YOU WANT A "GRAVESIDE" SERVICE AT YOUR SEA BURIAL? IF SO, WHAT KIND?

_____

_____

_____

WHERE ON THE WATER DO YOU WANT YOUR ASHES/BODY TO BE SCATTERED/INTERRED?

_____

_____

WHAT KIND OF BOAT AND HOW LARGE A BOAT DO YOU WANT?

_____

_____

Of all the military bugle calls, none is so easily recognized or more apt to render emotion than "Taps." Up until the Civil War, the traditional call at day's end was a tune, borrowed from the French, called "Lights Out." In July 1862, in the aftermath of the bloody Seven Days battles and the loss of 600 men, Union General Daniel Adams Butterfield called the brigade bugler to his tent. General Butterfield thought "Lights Out" was too formal, and he wished to honor his men with something more appropriate for Americans. That night he wrote the twenty-four-note tune "Taps," which was soon adopted by Union and Confederate brigades. It was officially recognized by the U.S. Army in 1874 and became the standard at military funeral ceremonies in 1891. It's believed that the name *Taps* comes from the three drum taps that were played as a signal for "lights out" when a bugle wasn't used.

COME TO
THE CREMATION

Believe it or not, your family can be there for a small service just prior to your body being pushed into the crematorium. Although it may sound a bit odd, your loved ones might feel a need to do this, and you should be open to such requests. We've heard accounts of large groups of Japanese mourners pulling out their cell phones and grabbing shots of the body in a coffin as it slid into the crematorium. Now, that's entertainment!

DO YOU WANT YOUR LOVED ONES THERE AS YOUR BODY IS PLACED INTO THE CREMATORIUM? IS THERE A SPECIAL PRAYER, PASSAGE, OR POEM THAT YOU WISH TO HAVE SPOKEN THEN?

_____

_____

_____

Carmen has been adopted by many mothers over the years. One of them, Kate, had a strong tie to the "other side" and harbored a huge crush on the *Star Trek* character Dr. McCoy. The first entry in her will asked that her relatives cremate her, buy a life-size cardboard cutout of Dr. McCoy, and send her ashes out, on top of the cardboard McCoy, into her beloved Gulf of Mexico. As Kate's ashes floated out to sea on the good doctor's chest, a large wave hit them and decapitated McCoy, effectively terminating the mission. Carmen sees this as one of the great weekends of her life, one she will never forget. Remember our motto: nothing is too over the top!

One last thing your family should consider for any graveside service you choose is to bring your pet, where allowed, if you want to. We truly believe that pets are certified members of the family and that the people attending your service will benefit tremendously from the comfort of a happy dog or contented cat. Pets have feelings and deeply rooted instincts, so they should be able to share in the grief and exaltation of your final good-byes, also (and spread some good cheer, as only pets can!)

MORE THOUGHTS ON GRAVESIDE SERVICES:

_____
_____
_____
_____
_____
_____
_____
_____
_____
_____
_____
_____
_____
_____
_____
_____
_____
_____
_____
_____
_____
_____
_____
_____
_____
_____
_____
_____
_____
_____
_____
_____
_____

CHAPTER 9

THE FUNERAL ❋ AND ❋ MEMORIAL SERVICES

LIGHTS, CAMERAS, ACTION!
—THE MAIN EVENT

The funeral, the memorial, the homecoming—whatever you want to call it—this is the service that honors you and addresses the reality of your death. You may be wondering: what is the difference between a funeral and memorial? That's easy—a funeral has your body (or what's left of it) somewhere in the vicinity, and a memorial does not. Both ceremonies usually cover the highlights of your life and tell your story in a condensed fashion.

Now, no one wants to say anything bad about the dead; it's an unwritten law—well, we say bunk! If you don't make others aware that you want to be talked about as you really were, then there will be no feeling, there will be no connection; the service will be shallow and empty. Tell people who will be speaking at your ceremony not to be so polite about who you were—tell them to be honest. Being merely polite about the deceased at this time is like pasting a smiley face on the Pieta. It doesn't acknowledge the richness, depth, complexity, and beauty of life.

You can choose the various elements that define who you were and what your life was about. This can be a production that includes an introduction, music, stories, quotes, video, and religious or spiritual elements. It can be traditional or totally unorthodox or a mix of both. Tradition has it that the service is supposed to provide a loving and positive remembrance of the deceased, but one person's loving memoriam can be another person's worst nightmare. If you're worried about having a sappy and untruthful service, now is the time to make sure that doesn't happen.

We think it's very important to set a tone and keep it in mind as you plan your funeral or memorial service. There are many ways to accomplish this. For instance, look at the difference between these three statements:

❖ "He was a wonderful father and husband."

❖ "He was a wonderful father, husband, and generous to a fault; in fact, he gave all our money to a wonderful charity—Caesar's Palace. It soothed the souls of millions."

❖ "He loved being a dad, a husband, a pain in the ass, and most of all he loved the Day's Inn for an anonymous 'time-out.'"

The service should be respectful, but you can define what that is. It can be anything: solemn (Bible passages), funny (stories about how you made someone laugh), sweet (a first grade poem with a first grade photo), over the top (fireworks and skydivers), soulful (bagpipes playing "Amazing Grace"), bittersweet ("My mom married my boyfriend, so he became her husband and my wonderful stepfather—and later my lover again!"), adoring ("I didn't know it was possible to love someone this much"), goofy and silly (at an amusement park or with a conga line), angry and spiteful ("I should have been in the hall of fame!"), joyous (an authentic New Orleans jazz funeral), or irreverent (a stripper-gram and a mime). It can be long or short (epic poem or haiku), soft or loud. It can even be a multimedia experience. Now is the time to plan your service because it's one of the very few times that you'll ever have such a captive and receptive audience focused solely on you.

WHAT ARE YOUR INITIAL THOUGHTS ON THE TYPE OF
FUNERAL SERVICE YOU WANT?

_____

_____

_____

_____

Before we move on, here are some questions to consider:

❖ Do you even want a service?

❖ If you don't really want one and your family and friends do, would you be agreeable? No matter what you say, they may do one anyway, so why not give them some suggestions?

❖ If you want a service, do you want to contribute financially to the planning? (You don't need to feel obligated or guilty about this—you'll be dead.)

If you want to leave it up to your loved ones and you don't want to participate in any way, then you may want to skip to the next chapter.

WHERE DO YOU WANT IT?

Well, you're still here, so we're assuming you want to have a service and you want to help plan it. Now for the location. We'll try to make it easier for you by suggesting lots of options:

❖ PLACES OF WORSHIP: a church, temple, mosque, Quaker meeting house, cathedral, Kingdom Hall, megachurch, synagogue.

❖ SAFE AND FAMILIAR PLACES: a friend's home, your home, your parent's home, old folks home, a rooftop, garden, backyard, movie theater, ballpark, playground, the Elk's Club, Rotary Club, Kiwanis Club, coffee shop, bingo hall, health club, local bar, a dock, bowling alley, town square, the library, a barn, corral.

❖ PLACES THAT UPLIFT YOU: the beach, woods, forest, national park, civic park, state park, lake, stream, country road, mountaintop, desert, botanical garden, rock garden, valley.

❖ AN ISLAND: St. Barts, the Florida Keys, Jamaica, Bermuda, St. Thomas, St. Croix, Puerto Rico, Long Island, Catalina Island, Puget Sound, St. Simon's Island, Block Island, Campobello Island, Hawaii, Tahiti, Fiji, Aleutian Islands, The Maldives, Capri, Sicily, the Green Islands, Manhattan, Staten Island, Coney Island, Alcatraz.

❖ SOMETHING ELSE, PERHAPS: a boat, ferry, museum, riding stable, music hall, historical site, sports arena, department store (last-minute shopping, anyone?), theater, aquarium, zoo, classroom, pool hall, school auditorium, mall, university campus, amusement park, top of a tall building (doom with a view), a firehouse, cathouse, casino, vineyard, reptile farm, auction house, on board a tour bus of your favorite city, an amusement park, spa, rollercoaster, airplane, restaurant.

WHERE DO YOU WANT YOUR FUNERAL SERVICE TO BE?

_____

_____

WHOM DO YOU WANT TO SPEAK?

Once you've picked the location, it's time to decide who you want to conduct and speak at the service. This is an honor for whomever you choose, and it's not to be taken lightly. Remember, if you choose a family member or close friend to speak at your service, you might want to consider the difficulty of such a request—they'll be grieving and possibly too distraught or emotional to participate. The closer to you, the more difficult—but don't let that stop you from making the request. Some suggestions: religious or spiritual leader, family member, friend, spouse of a close friend or family member, in-law, family friend, co-worker, distant but significant relative or friend, civic leader, church member, doctor, sponsor, lawyer, teammate, neighbor, teacher, school principal, member or leader of a club, member or leader of a volunteer group, coach, neighbor, boss, therapist. You might not want to pick an ex-wife, an illegitimate child, your wife's divorce attorney, your bookie, or the friend you go to brothels with. Then again, you might.

Speaking at a funeral/memorial service can be extremely difficult and very uncomfortable if people are not used to speaking in front of crowds, so start thinking about it now. When you're choosing whom you want to speak about you, consider people who are capable of public speaking, but don't make your decision based solely on their comfort level. A raw, messy, heartfelt testimonial is completely appropriate here and will be quite moving. Once you make a choice or two, we recommend having a discussion about whether they're interested in doing it and what you would like them to say. You may even want to write their passages. That can be a relief to some people. On the other hand, you can push a loved one just a bit beyond their comfort level, and that can work as well. Encourage friends and family to prepare their statements in advance, since they may be too distraught to write something after you're gone. Don't forget children as speakers; they can be amazing. In our experience, many kids accept death more readily than adults.

WHOM DO YOU WANT TO CONDUCT THE SERVICE? WHY?

_____

_____

WHO ELSE DO YOU WANT TO SPEAK AT THE SERVICE?

_____

_____

Words are usually the heart of the ceremony. So don't hold back; this is the last time you'll have to tell everyone what you think.

WHAT DO YOU WANT TO SAY?

This is the time to help friends and loved ones remember you the way you want to be remembered. Don't worry about being embarrassed—you'll be dead! It may be the only time in your life that you get this opportunity. You can accomplish many things with thoughts such as these:

❊ You can thank people.

❊ You can tell them you love them.

❊ You can reach out to estranged family, friends, colleagues, ex-spouses, or anyone you feel you've wronged.

❊ You can set the record straight.

❊ You can apologize for perceived or actual wrongs.

❊ You can reveal things about yourself—your secret charity work, good deeds, your deep spirituality or religiosity (who knew you were a Zoroastrian?), your hopes and dreams, your disappointments, that you're really a man or a woman, that you never liked living in the suburbs, that you're a closet Republican.

❊ You can share stories about things that gave you great joy—people, animals, sports teams, vacations, books, art, television shows, music, theater, activities, shopping (sales in particular), meals and food, parties, nature, homes, the five senses, living in the city, etc.

❊ You might want to reveal a few secrets—how well the witness protection program worked for you, your criminal record, your sex-change operation, your illegitimate children, your adventures in polygamy, your unrequited love, hidden money, the most embarrassing moments of your life, your spiritual revelations, etc.

This is where Chapter Two comes in handy. If you've filled it in, it will be a wonderful resource for the people who will be speaking at your service.

WHAT DO YOU WANT TO BE SAID ABOUT YOU PERSONALLY?

_____

_____

_____

_____

WHAT DO YOU WANT THEM TO SAY?

You've planned your say. Now it's time for your family and friends to say things about you that they love, to give their own personal stories about you or to say things they've been too reserved or shy to express. These testimonials can be planned or spontaneous. Beware: the spontaneous testimonials can be deadly, given the circumstances. Without preparation, many times people run on and on and say nothing of significance. But give them permission to open up and let them know that they can't get into any trouble, regardless of what they say. Many times this opening up on the part of friends and loved ones can facilitate important healing.

Here are some hints on how you can help family and friends recall memories for their testimonials:

❉ Look at photographs together and find out what memories and feelings are awakened.

❉ Carry a pen and small notebook with you—you never know when something will inspire you.

❉ Reread old letters and post cards together. This is very powerful.

❉ Pay attention to feelings and memories evoked by smells, foods, music, holidays and seasons.

Major subject matter for testimonials can include events from your childhood, milestones in your career, or things such as where you were or what you were doing when a famous person died, when astronauts first landed on the moon, when the Red Sox won the World Series, etc. They can talk about your family (or lack thereof), the side of you that people didn't know, what it was like to travel with you, experiences while shopping or playing sports or other favorite activities that you shared, a challenging time in your life that was handled well, your God-given gifts (talents and personality traits), examples of how you used them and how people were affected by them.

You probably have inspired and helped people in a number of extraordinary ways. Tell people this is a good time to let you know that—while you're still alive. Remember, humor can be a very uplifting, life-affirming part of the service. People may want to share a big faux pas that you made, an embarrassing but hilarious moment, charming quirks, a ridiculous dream or aspiration, an influence (positive or negative) you had on them, how you spoke and communicated with people, what your sense of humor was like, pet stories, their stories of your children or relatives, and so forth.

Other great possibilities for you to incorporate into your service are readings from:

❉ FICTION—classics, contemporary, foreign, humorous, mystery, fantasy, science fiction, romance, adventure. Go online and search for "literary quotes" or search by an author's name or subject. Try Amazon.com, Barnesandnoble.com and Google Books for lists and excerpts.

❖ RELIGIOUS TEXTS—The Bible, the Qur'an, the Bhagavad-Gita, The Talmud, the teachings of Confucius, The Dead Sea Scrolls, the Blue Cliff Record, The Book of Mormon, the Upanishads, the Vedas, Tipitaka, etc.

❖ SPIRITUAL BOOKS— *Conversations with God* by Neale Donald Walsch, *Tuesdays With Morrie* books by Mitch Albom, *A Course of Miracles*, Eckhart Tolle books, Paul Coelho books, *Chicken Soup For the Soul* by Jack Canfield and Mark Victor Hansen, *Way of the Peaceful Warrior* by Dan Millman, *Many Lives, Many Masters* by Brian Weiss, Sylvia Brown books, Florence Scovel Schinn books, *Into the Light* by Dannion Brinkley, Tibetan Book of the Dead, *Life After Life* by Raymond Moody, *The Purpose Driven Life* by Rick Warren, *Between Death and Life* by Dolores Cannon.

❖ CHILDREN'S BOOKS— Fairy tales are great! Or *The Little Prince* by Antoine de Saint-Exupéry; *Charlotte's Web* by E. B. White, *The Runaway Bunny* by Margaret Wise Brown, *Winnie-the-Pooh* by A. A. Milne, *The Jungle Book* by Graham C. Barrett, *Alice In Wonderland* by Lewis Carroll, *The Wizard of Oz* by L. Frank Baum.

❖ POETRY—epic, haiku, ballad, elegy, nursery rhymes, limericks

❖ PHILOSOPHY—the Greeks, the Germans, the French, the Chinese, the Naturalists

❖ HISTORY, MEMOIRS, BIOGRAPHIES, SCIENCE BOOKS

❖ MOVIES—you can go online to www.imdb.com or www.moviequotes.com for inspiration.

❖ TELEVISION—the classics, the personalities, the series and miniseries, the talk shows, the comedies, the news programs

❖ PLAYS—Shakespeare, of course.

❖ SONG LYRICS—Use lyrics from Broadway shows, pop hits from your teenage years, operas, standards, chants, jingles, TV show openings. A couple of possibilities: "Blackbird" by the Beatles and "Every Time We Say Goodbye" by George Gershwin.

❖ MAGAZINES AND NEWSPAPERS—use headlines or significant events (political events and movements, scientific discoveries, social achievements or failures, battle of the sexes, advice columns); take things from the year you were born or from another significant year—when you got married, the birth of your first child, your first divorce, you last face lift, the time you got run over by a car and met that cute doctor in the emergency room.

You can also have them use quotes from your teachers, parents, grandparents, even historical figures from saints to sinners to whatever.

SETTING UP THE BONES (SO TO SPEAK) OF YOUR SERVICE

Now's the time to organize and think about the structure of the service, but don't let this cramp your creativity and vision. Think in terms of opening statements, eulogy, testimonials, and closing statements or thoughts.

You can do the traditional opening statement: "We've gathered here in this place to mourn . . . " This is a safe choice because it lets people know they're in the right place at the right time. A nontraditional opening would be: "Anybody got a corkscrew, or feel they've been screwed?"

Start the ceremony itself with the eulogy. Since this is a laudatory speech or written tribute, especially one praising someone who has died, you might want someone else to write this. You may contribute some material, if you wish. Designate a friend or family member to be involved, either or as a writer or editor. Make sure this person knows you very well. After the eulogy come the testimonials from family and friends and sometimes coworkers and others.

If your eulogy or testimonials are written in advance, ask if you may read them. What a gift it would be to hear what your friends and family will say about you after you're gone. Isn't that everyone's fantasy—to be at their own funeral and hear what everyone will be talking about?

Last come the closing words. This includes some of the same ingredients as the body of the service. Remember, this is the last thought or impression of you that people will take away with them. Choose carefully, but don't restrict yourself. The closing can be a story, parable, joke, demand, poem, scripture, or prayer.

Another option to consider is a good-bye letter. After all, why should suicide survivors get all the good letters? Some of the most beautiful letters are composed during difficult times. Why should that be the only time that people get these kinds of letters? Let's create a new tradition where these letters are a natural part of saying good-bye. It's like taking the tradition back from pain. When people commit suicide, they usually know when they are going to die, therefore they can take the time to write what they want. The importance of writing a letter now before you die is that you have the time and wherewithal to do it. This is a very personal choice; it's not an obligation. So, if you're up to it, do it.

Take the liberty to fully express yourself. For some of us it's harder to say the heartfelt things to those closest to us. This is the perfect time to open up about your deepest feelings. Think of it as saying good-bye to your friends. If you can talk, then you can write. It can even be a stream-of-consciousness letter. Just get your thoughts down on paper—whatever you say will be a gift to those you leave behind. Let's get started on a rough draft:

OPENING:

_____

_____

_____

_____

_____

_____

EULOGY:

_____
_____
_____
_____
_____

PRAYERS:

_____
_____
_____
_____
_____

TESTIMONIALS/REMINISCENCES:

_____
_____
_____
_____
_____

PASSAGES/TEXTS/POEMS/QUOTES:

_____
_____
_____
_____
_____

ANYTHING OUT OF THE ORDINARY?

_____
_____
_____

FINAL PASSAGES/STATEMENT/WORDS:

_____

_____

_____

_____

_____

GOOD-BYE LETTER:

_____

_____

_____

_____

You might want to match each of these sections with a person. That person could even be you, recorded and sounding live. What an amazing experience for family and loved ones to hear your voice after you're gone! Your voice was your instrument, your tonal signature, and it carries a great depth of emotion. You can read short pieces from books or longer passages from scripture or something you've written specifically for the funeral, like saying good-bye and that you love them all. Today it's so easy to record things, so there's nothing to hold you back. You could say things occasionally throughout the service, or perhaps even better, completely take them by surprise at the very end. So simple and yet so powerful. Loop yourself repeating a phrase or combining phrases, like: "Thank you," "I love you," "Bless you," "See you later," "Signing off, this is [your name here]," "See you on the other side!" "I'm not kidding!" "Holy cow!" . . . whatever. Funny or poignant or profane—everything works here.

MUSIC

Your music choices are very important and deserve some thought. Music is evocative, it tells a great deal about you, and it is a powerful mood setter. It can easily energize an audience, uplift them, and take them on a roller coaster of emotions. Make it a wild ride, and don't limit yourself in your choices. Try things you never thought would be appropriate for a funeral or memorial. People love the unexpected.

Go crazy in planning and selecting your music—just jump in and take the plunge! The process is so fulfilling. It's about your life, your heart, your soul. You will probably find yourself on a roller-coaster ride. Almost any music takes on increased meaning and complexity and is layered with wonderful nuances in this context. Certain music can make it more like a celebration than a service—so choose the music to fit the mood you want to set.

Here are a few examples of songs that give you a sense of the range of possibilities. Some songs have several versions with different artists performing them, so try out different versions to see which one fits best:

❖ SAD (The aria from "La Boheme" by Puccini; "I'll Be Seeing You," which has over eighty different recorded versions; "I'll Stand By You" by Carrie Underwood)

❖ SENTIMENTAL ("As Time Goes By," Herman Hupfeld; Louis Armstrong's "What a Wonderful World"; the "flying" section of the *Out of Africa* soundtrack.)

❖ UPLIFTING ("Love Train" by The O'Jays; "Water Music" by Handel; "We Are Family" by Sister Sledge)

❖ JUBILANT ("When the Saints Go Marching In," almost any version; "You Are the Sunshine of My Life" by Stevie Wonder)

❊ HUMOROUS ("Is That All There Is?" by Peggy Lee; "Live and Let Die" by Paul McCartney; "Respect" by Aretha Franklin—especially if you've been beaten down your whole life!)

❊ HOPEFUL ("The Impossible Dream" from *Man of La Mancha*; "Something In the Air" by Thunderclap Newman; "Tomorrow" from *Annie*)

❊ THE PERSONAL TOUCH (If you're lucky enough to be named Johnny or Gloria or Baby, there are a zillion songs to choose from.)

❊ REFLECTIVE ("Blackbird" and many others by the Beatles; "Face of Love" by Eddie Vedder; "Claire de Lune" by Claude Debussy; "Midnight Train to Georgia" by Gladys Knight and the Pips)

❊ TENDER ("Layla" by Eric Clapton; "Until You Come Back to Me" by Aretha Franklin; "Nothing Compares 2 U" by Sinead O'Conner)

❊ IMPASSIONED ("Break On Through to the Other Side" by the Doors; "Wild Horses" by the Rolling Stones; an Astor Piazzola ballad; "Transcendental Blues" by Steve Earle)

❊ SUICIDAL ("Strange Fruit" by Billy Holliday; "Gloomy Sunday" by Artie Shaw; "Adagio in G Minor" by Albinoni)

❊ COUNTRY ("I Go Out Walking After Midnight" by Patsy Cline; "Drop Kick Me, Jesus, Through the Goal Post of Life" by Paul Craft; "We'll Meet Again" by Johnny Cash)

❊ CONTEMPLATIVE (Symphoniae by Hlidegard Von Bingen; "Danny Boy" by Elvis Presley; "Wings," the *Brokeback Mountain* theme song, by Gustavo Santaolalla; Symphony No.7 in A Major by Ludwig von Beethoven)

❊ SWEET ("Somewhere Over the Rainbow" by Harold Arlen; "God Only Knows" by the Beach Boys)

❊ SOULFUL ("Old Man River" from *Showboat*; "Both Sides Now" by Joni Mitchell; "With a Little Help From My Friends" by Joe Cocker)

❖ RIP YOUR GUTS OUT ("Every Time We Say Goodbye" by Cole Porter—Annie Lenox has a great version; "I'm So Lonesome I Could Cry" by Hank Williams; "When a Man Loves a Woman" by Percy Sledge)

❖ TOTALLY UNEXPECTED (Bulgarian Women's Choir; "Lullaby and Goodnight"; a Gene Krupa drum solo; anything by Miles Davis; "Happy Talk" from *South Pacific*; Whirling Dervishes)

When it comes to the kind of music you select, you may mix it up or stay with a theme. You can have recorded music or live performances or a combination; all are very compelling. We saw eleven men at our friend's father's memorial sing fraternity songs during his service, and it was a wonderful tonic; they sang life back into a very solemn group. Everybody was captivated. At another funeral we attended, The Gospel at Colonus choir sang songs from the show while moving through the congregation, ending up at the front of the church. Everyone was clapping and laughing and crying along.

Here are some more types of music and sounds to consider: choir, organ, piano, jazz band, individual musician, gospel, blues, standards, big band, string quartet, barbershop quartet, a cappella, opera, classical, hymns, chants, rap, rock, country, Broadway musicals, movie soundtrack music, TV themes, commercial jingles, patriotic anthems, holiday, klezmer, new age, Christian, Sufi, electronic, African drums, ragtime, reggae, Motown, salsa, classical guitar, Native American, disco, lullabies, Japanese drums or flute, waltz, marching music, school songs, childhood songs, flamenco, Yiddish theater, metal, pop, team songs, gypsy, folk songs, spirituals, Appalachian tunes, Irish ballads, or nature sounds and sound effects (whale songs, bird songs, rain, ocean waves, rivers running, waterfalls, fog horns, cicadas, babies cooing, coyotes howling, wolves, owls, lightening, thunder, wind).

It may be the sounds of something you loved or a signature sound—a sporting event, sounds from home videos of your children, pet sounds like barks or meows or your parrot's favorite sayings, a passage from your favorite books on tape, your voice mail recording or your unique cell phone ringtone. You can even have a personal symphony composed by music professors or a talented friend. Go ahead and rewrite the lyrics to your favorite songs from musicals, standards, or pop songs. The sky's the limit.

Once you've chosen the music and/or sounds, it's time to determine how it will work in your service. Let's break it out:

MUSIC/SOUND PLAYING AS THE GUESTS ENTER (DO YOU WANT THEM TO MEDITATE, CHAT, LISTEN TO FUNNY LYRICS, SOB?):

_____

_____

MUSIC/SOUND TO OPEN THE SERVICE (THIS WILL SET THE TONE):

_____

_____

INTERLUDE (WILL THIS BE CONTEMPLATIVE OR PART OF THE TRIBUTE TO YOU?):

_____

_____

CLOSING THE SERVICE (SUM IT UP):

_____

_____

RECESSIONAL (WHAT WILL PEOPLE HEAR AND HUM AS THEY WALK OUT?):

_____

_____

CLOSING RITUAL

A closing ritual is something else to consider— it's a ritual that gives form to feeling. In this case it's feelings about you and your life. Think in terms of physical manifestations or symbols of your being—something simple that they can carry with them. It gives them something to hold on to, literally. We picture a table set up by the door as people leave the venue. Some ideas for closing rituals:

✷ If you are a sports nut, you could give out a ball from your favorite game or a hat from your favorite team.

✷ If you love nature, how about a bowl full of shells, rocks, crystals, feathers, leaves, or something you were especially fond of?

✷ People could also perform an action that holds significance in your life, such as ringing a bell, striking a gong, beating a drum, lighting a candle, taking a packet of seeds, taking a spin on a roulette wheel—something that's quick and won't jam up traffic.

✷ A very simple parting shot is to have everyone write a few words in a guest book on the way out (if they haven't written anything on the way in). Keep it informal, loose, and fun, or what they write won't mean anything. Encourage people to be spontaneous. Perhaps you can buy the book in advance and write a note on every page, such as, "Thanks for coming!," "Have a good day!," "Miss me?," "Don't worry, I'm happy," "How'd you like the show? Just because it closed on the same day it opened doesn't mean it was bad!" This would definitely be like an encounter with you and could be quite startling.

✷ Everyone can take a drink from a paper shot glass. This says you were very intoxicating!

WHAT "RITUAL OF YOU" WOULD YOU LIKE AT VERY END OF THE CEREMONY?

_____

_____

You could even play a videotape consisting of photos and/or video of your life—growing up, favorite moments, favorite people, life passages, favorite places, clips from favorite movies or TV shows, or even your own video goodbye. It could be a collage of your life all set to your favorite music. Don't fret about this—it should be fun. It's all about your life.

If you want to continue the media experience, have a live webcast of the entire ceremony. It's not so expensive, it just requires contacting a webcast company or talking to your funeral director. (Internet search: "webcasts for funerals.") Is Grandma too old to travel? Is someone you know eight months pregnant or housebound? It's not uncommon to do live webcasts of a birth, especially for soldiers in Iraq and Afghanistan. Get your family to send out e-mail announcements or invite people through the mail!

DO YOU WANT A VIDEOTAPE OF SOME SORT PLAYING AT THE END AS PEOPLE WALK OUT? IF SO, WHAT KIND?

_____

_____

HOW ABOUT A LIVE WEBCAST?

_____

_____

The idea in planning your funeral/memorial service is to create an experience that reflects the individuality of the person being honored—which is you! Everyone is unique; no one's life is mundane. Even if you think your life was uneventful and not that meaningful, it certainly wasn't to the people who care about you. This can be an opportunity for you to create a new tradition that adds to or reinterprets the more traditional ways of coping with death and celebrating life!

MORE THOUGHTS ON THE FUNERAL AND MEMORIAL SERVICE:

_____

_____

_____

_____

_____

_____

_____

_____

_____

_____

_____

_____

_____

_____

_____

_____

_____

_____

_____

_____

_____

_____

_____

_____

_____

_____

_____

_____

_____

_____

_____

_____

_____

CHAPTER 10

THE REHEARSAL DINNER

YOU REALLY CAN ATTEND YOUR OWN FUNERAL... SORT OF

I sn't it everyone's fantasy to attend their own funeral? Wouldn't you like to witness all the grieving and hear all the wonderful things people will say about you? Well, don't wait until you're dead! You can celebrate your life while you're still alive and kicking, and you won't have to pretend to be a ghost behind the curtains to hear those glowing compliments.

We have wondered why people spend great time, effort, and money to come to "visit" you once you're dead. It just doesn't make sense. Why not come to visit while you're alive and can really appreciate it. Of course, death happens quickly sometimes, and it's not possible to do this. However, there are a great many opportunities for people to come when you're feeling well enough, even though you may be dying.

Imagine being in those circumstances and throwing yourself a party beforehand and seeing your kids, your grandkids, your friends, and neighbors while you are alive. Plus, all of them would be together in happier circumstances, and their memory of you would not be of a corpse, but of a living, breathing person. Just think how many people say after seeing their loved one as a corpse: "I wish that wasn't my last image of them." Well, then, don't make it the last glimpse. These pre-passing parties would be opportunities for people to say things that they normally postpone or don't think about until after you've died. People are more open to expressing love and are more open to healing in these end-of-life situations.

Everyone wins here. You win because you enjoy the comfort and support of your family and friends one last time. You hear things that perhaps you've never heard before and can understand how people loved and appreciated you. They win because they get the chance to say those things, and they won't have any of the regrets or guilt that can eat people up. Great healing can come from these opportunities.

That doesn't mean it will happen, but the possibility exists. And you increase your chances of realizing that potential if you have the rehearsal. Seems logical, doesn't it? So why don't people do it more often? We can only think it's cultural and even subconscious, because people somehow place more importance on paying their respects after you've died. What's more respectful than honoring the living? This is a pattern in our society—to say we're not just tossing the bodies away. But people can feel shamed for not going to the funeral, and yet somehow it's okay not to visit while someone is sick and dying. Okay, sometimes sick people aren't good company, since they feel and often look like crap, but does that matter? A visit means everything to the dying, even if they can't express that.

There's a lot of evidence that people can hear and comprehend things when they're unconscious and near death. We're urging people to stop and think about this a bit. We say plan it now so that, circumstances allowing, you will have the great opportunity to hear all those wonderful compliments while you're alive. We're not saying that we think funerals aren't important. We believe it's extremely important for the living to come together and mourn and share their grief. But we also think there's a knee-jerk fear and embarrassment in the presence of death and sickness, which can keep people from coming to terms with you and your passing before you're gone.

So, why not call them on this resistance and just throw yourself a party before you get too sick? How can they not come under the circumstances? There aren't many acceptable excuses in this case. Coming after you're dead is supported by the culture, but if you tell your boss that your aunt is sick and may be dying, you won't necessarily get time off from work to pay her a visit. Yet, if you say your aunt has died, most likely they understand and give you the time off to go to the funeral. Even airlines give "bereavement fares"—hefty discounts so people can attend funerals—but they won't offer discounts if you're just near death. Weird, and yet at the same time it's understandable. But we say change the paradigm! We need everyone's agreement on this to change our cultural practices and traditions. You can help by planning your going away/rehearsal party now!

WHAT DO YOU WANT AT YOUR "LAST SUPPER"?

We do think that, although you are technically planning the party in advance, you may want it to be potluck or catered or put together by a special friend who is willing and able. The last thing you want to do when you don't feel well is to throw a party, so we think the idea of the old-fashioned potluck meal is perfect, because of the symbolism that everyone is bringing a part of themselves and offering it to you as thanks for who you have been to them in their lives. People traveling from out of town won't be able to do this as easily, but it's the same gesture if you swing by the grocery store and the wine store and buy something. There's also a lot to be said for going out—no mess at home. Whatever you choose, just be sure to have lots of comfort food and refreshments to soothe the soul, get the emotional wheels turning, and free people, including you, to express intimate thoughts of love or anything else.

This is the no-holds-barred party where reconciliation can take place, the air can be cleared, and issues of loss and abandonment can be addressed directly with you (don't let them take it out on you, however!). Ideally, at the end of the party, you and others will feel great joy and relief and that bittersweet feeling that seems to sum up life itself. Life really can be sweetest at the end, so share that with others and it will increase your appreciation. This is truly a transitional party, and everyone is celebrating your life in the same way they would your graduation or any other important life-changing event.

Just remember, everybody is going to reconcile their life in one way another, and it's more powerful to do it in the here and now. This is for you and your loved ones, both in terms of karma and psychological peace of mind. This time can be compared to the Tibetan bardo, which means the transitional or in-between state. It's akin to getting your business affairs in order, but this is getting your emotional and spiritual affairs in order. Not that you need a party to do that, but in a festive atmosphere, it will feel more celebratory and be more conducive to transformation.

DO YOU WANT A REHEARSAL DINNER/PARTY IF YOU ARE WELL ENOUGH?

_____

_____

WHERE WOULD YOU LIKE TO HAVE IT?

_____

_____

WOULD YOU LIKE IT TO BE POTLUCK OR CATERED OR AT A RESTAURANT?

_____

_____

Note: it would be fun to make up invitations well in advance that you can complete when the proper time comes. You could have an image of a photo of your older hand on the front of the card. You can contrast it with your baby hand on the "cover" or put your baby photo inside. Imagine what you can do with an invitation for your life's party—the photos, the thoughts written by you, or the passages quoted—what an emotional wallop!

Also, the rehearsal party is a perfect time for giving away special keepsakes that you want people to have. Jewelry, clothing, hats, books, CDs, photos, prized possessions, boat, house, sports car—the sky's the limit. Think of how nice this would be for you and your loved ones. You can have the satisfaction of seeing them receive your gifts, which most likely will have powerful resonance of feeling and meaning.

So go ahead and make some notes about the party and what you want to do. Start making a guest list and a menu and designing your invitation now—we guarantee it will be fun! Talk with your loved ones and see if this whole idea doesn't inspire lively conversations and a desire for them to participate in the planning. Think of "bridesmaids and groomsmen" gifts—only this time for the people you've been "married" to your whole life: close friends and family. They'll be walking down the aisle with you at the funeral, so give them a little something in recognition of that. Maybe cufflinks and garters wouldn't be a good idea, but we love the gesture!

CHAPTER 11

THE FUNERAL ❊ OR ❊ MEMORIAL PARTY

IT'S MY PARTY AND I'LL DIE IF I WANT TO!

O kay, so now you're dead and everyone has said their good-byes—maybe in time, maybe not. And you've had your funeral, and you've wowed them with a fabulous production: the music! the lights! the oratory! the emotion! the flowers! the tears! the laughter! everyone looking thin and glamorous in black! They haven't seen a production like that since *Cat on a Hot Tin Roof* played at the freshman fair! Now for the final send-off party of your life.

This can range from a respectful remembrance to an all-out hullabaloo. If you want, this is where the fun can truly begin. Now is the time your loved ones get to eat, drink, and reminisce about you in an informal atmosphere. You are giving permission to your friends and family to grieve in their own way, whether that be quiet and introspective or loud and obnoxious. In many circles, death is considered to be the ultimate vacation and reward. Yes, people are mourning, but at the same time they are honoring your passing into a better world. If you and your family and friends believe in an afterlife, there is much to celebrate. If you don't believe in an afterlife, there is still much to celebrate: you.

Funeral and memorial parties are functions people attend only a handful of times in their lives. They are extraordinarily meaningful and filled with potential for an experience that provides a full range of emotions and thoughts. It is a mixture of pain and pleasure, tension and release, joy and sorrow, and it sums up the richness of life. Like the rehearsal party covered in the previous chapter, the funeral/memorial party is one of the few times people acknowledge and appreciate the gift of the bittersweet in life. It's like great food that you are unfamiliar with—it may seem odd to you and you have no context for it, but it's rich and fascinating, and it draws you to it and rewards you for your adventurous efforts.

Plan ahead for your funeral/memorial party and try to make sure there's enough money set aside in your estate to pay for it. That's not to say it has to be extravagant and expensive. Many families choose to have the memorial party at a later date when they feel better about things and when friends and loved ones from out of town have time to make travel arrangements. However, if you're having a funeral, you'll probably have to feed people following the service.

VENUES

Don't limit your thinking. Consider the expected and the unexpected, as both can be effective. We have a great list of venue ideas in the funeral and memorial services chapter. We suggest you go back and check out the list, come back here, and write down your choices in this section. Choose any place you celebrated life and felt wonderful about. Choose whatever fits in your budget and makes you happy to think about your loved ones enjoying. Why not have fun creating the best party you'll never attend?

VENUE CHOICE #1:

_____

_____

VENUE CHOICE #2:

_____

_____

VENUE CHOICE #3:

_____

_____

ATMOSPHERE

Identify the general atmosphere of the party you want to create: formal, informal, thematic, sit-down, cocktail-driven, all-out party (big blast), dark, light, ethereal, raucous, childlike, intimate, biker, tasteful, tasteless, ethnic, traditional . . . you get the idea. Think of the person being honored here (you) and then work from there. Were you a real stiff? Were you radical, a conformist, a cheerleader, atheistic, an athlete, against the norm? Try to fit the party to your personality or the fantasy of what you wanted to be. A theme properly chosen can answer all the questions about who, what, when, and where. Or you can combine themes to really throw everyone off.

WHAT KIND OF ATMOSPHERE/THEME DO YOU WANT FOR YOUR FUNERAL/MEMORIAL PARTY?

_____

_____

Do you want a party decorated or staged with items that were meaningful in your life? For example: your motorcycle, your guitar, your collection of shoes, collection of shells, sports equipment, favorite clothes, pom-poms, trophies, prom queen tiara, weights, bicycle, fireworks, fishing poles, gardening accoutrement, a map of the world with pins to show all the places you've been, a display of postcards of all the places you've been or wanted to go, international flags, a Christmas tree, angels, a collection of Christmas ornaments, stethoscopes, gavel, carpentry tools, nautical flags—things that reflected your passions, your profession, your secret fantasy, or your day-to-day life.

WHAT KINDS OF SPECIAL PROPS AND DECORATIONS
WOULD YOU LIKE AT THE PARTY?

_____

_____

PHOTOGRAPHS

These constitute the history and windows onto your life. They can be a road map to your life experiences: the people, places, events, and history. Think of photos placed in a collage, and don't worry about the order, positioning, or relevance of these pictures. However, you may want to tell the story of your life by presenting photos in chronological order. Both ways are valid. The total effect is what's important. It's a collection that makes a statement about your life. Images with you and your pets or your kids have particular impact. Or you can expand that idea to include photos showing you with your car, or you gardening, golfing, protesting a war, in a compromising position, at your prom, at your wedding, signing your divorce papers, in a mug shot, at the birth of your child, and so on—anything with strong emotional resonance.

Photos have historical significance, which adds to the richness of the total picture people have of you. It's a good idea to enlarge them, which can be done on a copy machine, in your computer, or at a local camera store. Wal-Mart or Sears can do this and do it cheaply.

Try putting the photos on poster board, large pieces of cardboard, or in oversized picture frames. They can be willy-nilly, linear, artistic, or thematic. Again, it's crucial to identify what you believe is important and follow that design and disregard any outmoded ideas of propriety—although we don't suggest naked photos! Try those digital photo frames in which a series of photos plays continuously one after the other. With the new computer photo programs, it's easy to make a slide show of your photos, complete with dissolves, music, and special effects and put them on a CD or a DVD.

ARE THERE SPECIFIC PHOTOS YOU WANT AT YOUR MEMORIAL?
WHICH ONES?

_____

_____

_____

_____

_____

_____

_____

_____

(We suggest noting them here, but you can also collect them in a notebook for easy access by your family.)

What about enlarging a full-length picture of you into a cardboard cutout? You can get one online for around $150. If you do it in advance, it's a clever decoration at your various passage-of-life parties. You will be right there at the door to greet everyone at the funeral/memorial party. The impact would be huge. Guests can have a picture made with "you." You could put a tape recorder behind your cutout and let the hilarity begin. Record some of your favorite phrases, put them on a recording device, and have them played back continuously. (Okay, take a break once in a while—it can be obnoxious.)

DO YOU WANT A LIFE-SIZED CARDBOARD CUTOUT OF YOU?
IF SO, WHICH PHOTO WOULD YOU LIKE TO USE?

_____

_____

FLOWERS

Flowers have been known to elevate the actual vibration of a room, which is one reason they are used to celebrate special occasions. There is only one rule: don't make them look like those big arrangements for winning horse races (unless for some reason, those big horseshoe designs have meaning for you.) Other than that, just use your favorite flowers. Cut out pictures of arrangements that you respond to from magazines and save them. Flowers have both personal and symbolic meaning. On the Internet there are lots of sites where you can go to learn about the symbolic meanings of flowers. They're fascinating.

Perhaps branches and sticks and leaves would be a good choice for decoration, depending on the season. Look around outside and see what's blooming. Like many things these days, less can be more when it comes to flowers at funerals. Plus there's always the carbon footprint to consider when shipping exotic flowers from far away. Some people don't even want flowers; they prefer that the money be spent in other ways. In fact, more and more people are requesting donations to their favorite charity or organization in lieu of flowers. Be sure to include that information in your obituary. You could request that people plant a tree in your name. It's a very popular gift for Jewish people to have a tree planted in Israel. Balloon bouquets with printed sentiments such as BON VOYAGE or GOOD LUCK or HAPPY TRAILS would be effective. SEE YOU SOON is something people may not want to see on a balloon message at your funeral party. However, SO LONG, SUCKERS would be a great ice-breaker.

WHAT KINDS OF FLOWERS WOULD YOU LIKE? WHICH FLORIST?

_____

_____

IN LIEU OF FLOWERS, TO WHICH CHARITY
WOULD YOU LIKE DONATIONS TO GO?

_____

_____

THE RECEPTION LINE

Isn't it odd how many parallels there are between weddings and funerals? For some people, weddings are the beginning of the end. You may wish to consider your funeral/memorial to be the end of the end. It may seem odd to have a reception line, but reception lines at funerals just happen naturally, so you may as well plan for it. We recommend putting strict limitations as to who is in the receiving line, because sometimes people think they're closer to you than they are. Our suggestion is that this is a short and sweet line; just the absolute closest family and maybe a friend or two. You don't want dozens of people waiting in line for fifteen minutes or longer to give their respects to people outside of your intimate circle. We were in a "reception" line at a friend's parent's funeral, and it moved at a glacial pace. We had to take turns waiting in line to pay our respects as we each raced to the bathroom because we couldn't afford to lose our place. So we say keep the line to a minimum; it's awkward and robs people of the time to enjoy everything you planned for the party. Don't worry about hurting anyone's feelings in selecting the reception line candidates. This is a day about you and not them.

DO YOU WANT A RECEPTION LINE?

_____

_____

WHO DO YOU WANT IN THE RECEPTION LINE (AND IN WHAT ORDER?)

_____

_____

FOOD:
Fine Dining for Fine Dying

Food is the staff of life and what better way to affirm life than to feed the people who have come to celebrate your time on Earth? Food is one of the best ways to experience the communion of life and relationships, and at funerals people often feel the need to break bread with their fellow grievers.

Funeral food tends to be the best food, since everybody's pulling out all the stops to help the bereaved family—or the worst because it was catered from a place nobody knew. So spend some time checking out restaurants, caterers, sandwich shops, pizza, whatever, so you can recommend whom to call. Not coincidentally, funeral food is also comfort food. At funerals people are giving and getting sustenance when they most need it. By planning the menu in advance, you are both feeding them metaphorically and helping your family in a very difficult time. Specific food always re-creates good memories from your life, and by using those recipes at your party, there can be great meaning behind the food that you've chosen.

Once again, designate someone to coordinate the food and drink. Choose a foodie—someone who knows great food and who knows and respects your tastes. You can have your friends bring their best dishes, organized by the "food coordinator," or you can choose your favorite recipes. If there was ever a time to forget about calories, carbs, and fat, this is it. Also, people will drink, so have the name and number of a taxi or car service readily available and even a little fund to pay for this, so people won't have any excuse to drink and drive. Another way to help out is to pay for some local hotel/motel rooms out of a party fund.

Make some notations about the food and drink that you want. Remember to make notes about brands, specifics (like what vintner and year of wine), and even recipes. Feel free to put your specifics, if they are many, on a separate piece of paper and tuck it into the back of this book. We have very specific recipes from our childhoods onward that we want people to use and experience, so we're going to leave those handy for our funeral party givers.

DRINKS:

_____

_____

APPETIZERS:

_____

_____

JUNK FOOD (CHIPS, DIPS, ETC.):

_____

_____

BREAD:

_____

_____

CHEESES:

_____

_____

SALADS AND SPREADS:

_____

_____

MAIN COURSE:

_____

_____

SIDE DISHES:

_____

_____

DESSERTS:

_____

_____

AFTER DINNER DRINKS:

_____

_____

CHILDREN'S DISHES:

_____

_____

This is the time to pull out all the stops. You don't have to do any of the work, so this can be as elaborate as you want. More and more people are hiring catering companies to handle the funeral party, which may be a good choice for you if you have the money. That way, people can just enjoy themselves and tell stories and get a little tipsy without having to toil in the kitchen. There are also armies of friends and neighbors ready to step in and help at any time. Some people prefer to take care of this so they can skip the funeral service, if the party comes right after the funeral. In the South, it is almost a ritual for a few of the deceased's best friends to stay at home during the service and help with the food, drink a little alcohol, and protect the silver.

Consider the food/drink presentation in terms of paper plates, plastic cups, fine china, everyday china, a combination of both, glassware, crystal, silverware, linens or paper napkins, tablecloth, and placement in the home or venue. Of course if it's catered, this decision is simplified. A great idea is to put a small card identifying the food and, if applicable, who made the dish. Depending on the turnout, the venue, and the weather, plan the location and traffic movements around the food and drink stations to avoid bottlenecks so people can keep moving. Plan it so people can mingle easily and at the same time avoid certain people—for example: ex-wives or husbands, the disenfranchised, loudmouths, room-clearers, in-laws, out-laws, ex-business partners, and solicitors of all kinds (i.e., life insurance salesmen—what a perfect place to pump the crowd). If you're worried about your friends and family using your party as a networking venue, you might choose to put tasteful, simple signs around the house, such as THE HOUSE HAS BEEN SOLD or NO SOLICITATIONS ON THE PREMISES.

GLASSWARE:

_____

_____

CRYSTAL PIECES:

_____

_____

PLATES:

_____

_____

LINENS:

_____

_____

TABLEWARE:

_____

_____

In lieu of a large party, your preference may be to have an intimate sit-down meal at your favorite restaurant, possibly paid for by you, or a quiet repast at your home. This, too, can be potluck, catered, take-out, fast food, lowbrow, or high brow. It can be breakfast, brunch, lunch, tea, supper, dinner, hors d'oeuvres and drinks, late-night cocktails and caviar, or early morning mimosas.

AUDIO/VIDEO PRESENTATION:
Catch me while you can

Don't be intimidated by the technical stuff. If you have a camera, a video cameras, or a disposable camera, you'll be fine. If the idea of this does become overwhelming, skip this section or assign someone who likes this stuff to be your audio/video/photo "executor." Think about weddings when they have those tapes where everyone sends the newlyweds their best wishes, then multiply the poignancy factor by about fifty, and you have some idea how moving a good-bye tape or a photo collection of you can be for your loved ones.

If you don't have someone in mind to handle this, designate someone to be the photographer or ask to set up a video camera in a quiet corner, with instructions for operation, and let the fun begin as people say whatever they want. It's like auditions for all those reality shows, but this time it's your reality show. Your family can dub the tapes, transfer digital footage to DVD, or have it done at a local photo store. Don't forget to arrange in advance for copying the photos to distribute to relatives and friends. Or tell them you plan to put the photos on a digital photo-sharing website like Flickr.com.

Using digital photography, your loved ones may want to create several copies of either hardbound or softbound photo books of the service and party. These books look completely professional and can be created easily with free programs from companies like Apple or Blurb.com online. You just pay for the number of books, according to size and the number of pages. Set up an account in advance with one of the many online stores that can print your books. They're actually quite reasonable, and you can even put them on the online store so that anyone can buy one, once they've been notified that they are available. Perhaps you want to designate a cover photo of yourself for the ultimate "book of you," a more inclusive book, which includes all your childhood and major-moment photos as well as ones from the various services and parties at the end of your life. This is a great new media service. Go to Blurb.com and look at a whole bookstore of professional-looking, but essentially homemade, books. The customer just fills in the text and photos in predetermined positions on the page and the company does the rest. Think how wonderful it would be for your loved ones to have a professional photo book of you after you're gone. Of course you can start planning the book now. You can even predetermine the placement of the photos and text, lay out the pages, and choose the cover—all before the funeral and memorial photos are added. You will have fun planning this one, that's a guarantee!

The more low-tech idea is to buy lots of disposable cameras and leave them around the room for guests to shoot photos, like they do at weddings. Some people will leave them for the family as requested, and some will take them home for their own enjoyment. Either is acceptable.

THE "ALTAR OF ME"

Really, it's nothing religious, but an "Altar of Me" may instead be a place where your family and friends display a collection of symbolic objects to evoke a personal remembrance of you—a place where people can take a few moments to honor you in their own way. This is the one time when we recommend you relinquish control. This is not about you remembering you; it's about your family and friends remembering you. Those who are inspired to do so can bring an object (ideally a small one) that reminds them of you and then take it home with them later if they want. Or your family can compile this from things all over your house. We know people have done this in smaller ways in the past, but we like the idea of a new tradition here—bring in a pile of stuff with a range of subjects—all related to you, of course. Bigger might be more of an impact here, but not necessarily.

Give your loved ones some guidance. Here are some suggestions for the altar of you: a photo of you with them, a menu from a great meal you had together, a playbill from a show you enjoyed together, a postcard from you, a souvenir from a trip or an outing or a major experience you had together, a favorite scent from a candle or soap or incense, a bottle of your favorite perfume or aftershave, a flower, a gift from them, a theater ticket, a baseball, a lugnut, a rock, a shell, bubble gum, some candy, money, a wooden spoon, fishing lures, a CD of your favorite music—anything that reminds them of you. More than likely you would be surprised if you could see what they brought. If you believe in the afterlife, then perhaps you will see it. But their choice will be totally subjective. In the end it's the cumulative effect of all these objects that will create an indelible memory of you. Be sure someone captures it in a photo.

TAKE-AWAY GOODIE BAGS

This is your personal goody bag of items that your loved ones can take away with them after the funeral/memorial that will remind them of you. This time you get to choose what represents you. It's a parting gift from you to them. Designate what you want in the goody bags (or good-bye bags) and arrange to have them placed on a table, perhaps by the entrance. Yes, someone (perhaps you) will have to put them together, but of course this can be done in advance very nicely. This is also a good idea for any party honoring you while you're alive, for example your seventieth birthday. Some suggestions: a favorite recipe, scrolls with favorite sayings or quotes, seeds of your favorite flowers or herbs or vegetables, favorite flower bulbs, a personalized postage stamp (check online for websites that make them), your all-time favorite photo of yourself, a small crystal or rock, a golf ball with your name on it, fishing lures, a CD of your favorite music, a playing card or a tarot card, chopsticks, incense, candles, postcards of favorite places, a lucky penny or dime, knitting needles, temporary tattoos, dominoes, dice, a lock of hair, a match, a cigarette, small bottles of alcohol, hand lotion, vitamins, toothpicks, a gift card to your favorite store—just about anything that fits within the size restrictions and screams "[your name here]"!

If you really want to go crazy and you have the funds, have your photo put on mugs, T-shirts, or calendars. We love the idea of a calendar with a new photo of you and a piece of advice or recipe each month. They won't forget you even if they try during that first year after you've gone. If this is something you really want to do, you may want to arrange it and pay for it in advance. Or not. But pass on the idea to them!

MORE THOUGHTS ON THE FUNERAL/MEMORIAL PARTY:

_____

_____

_____

_____

_____

_____

_____

_____

_____

_____

_____

_____

_____

_____

_____

_____

_____

_____

_____

_____

_____

_____

_____

_____

_____

_____

_____

_____

_____

_____

_____

_____

_____

_____

CHAPTER 12

GIVE 'EM THE BUSINESS

THE KIDNEYS, THE KIDS, AND THE COST OF THE COFFIN

T his may be the only chapter you really need to do. It is worth the time it takes to fill out as much of this information as you can. A few minutes now can save weeks of your loved ones' time, thousands of dollars, tons of heartache, and even someone's life (think organ and tissue donation).

In the United States, the management of wills and estates comes under the authority of each state's government. Rules, regulations, and procedures vary from state to state. Every county in the United States has a lawyers' association, and some of them offer low-fee counseling and are great at steering you in the right direction. The one big piece of advice the county lawyers' association gave us was to have everything notarized—without it your legal document could mean nothing. Notaries are easy to find in almost every town: banks, real estate offices, travel agencies, and other businesses that deal with legal documents for the public usually have a designated notary public on staff. And of course, have a lawyer double-check everything of a legal nature, if you can, especially your will.

Now is a good time to decide on an executor of your will, if you haven't designated one yet. The executor is the person in charge of taking care of your financial business once you are gone. They represent you in every way and essentially become you, in terms of making decisions after you've died. You might want to appoint a family member or a very close friend to take that role, since many executors are entitled to take two to four percent of the assets of the estate.

Is your will in order? If you don't want your executor to dig you up and stomp on you, make your will as simple as possible. Any thing or item listed in the will as going specifically to someone (i.e. "my porcelain Imani vase to my niece Kathy") must be appraised and listed as part of the estate. Make a list of what you want to give to whom, and leave it with your executor or in the envelope with your will. Also be sure that all your bank accounts have a cosigner, your insurance policies have a beneficiary, your investment monies have a beneficiary, and your retirement funds as well.

Anything that is jointly owned or has a beneficiary is "outside the will" and therefore not part of the estate for tax purposes. You can give up to two million dollars per person before they get taxed on it.

We suggest you make sure you have the following three documents. You can have a lawyer draw one up for a few hundred dollars or you can download each form from the Internet. Make sure you have them all notarized:

* Durable Power of Attorney: This allows you to designate who will handle your money decisions if you become incapacitated. If you have chosen an executor, you may not need this. Check with your lawyer.

* Durable Power of Attorney for Health Care: This lets you name who will make medical decisions for you if you're incapacitated—decisions like when to remove a feeding tube or pull the plug.

* A Living Will: This tells doctors exactly what kind of care you do and don't want to receive if you're terminally ill and incapacitated. Keep signed copies of this in your car and your house so paramedics won't perform extraordinary procedures to keep you alive, if that is your desire.

You also need to designate someone to carry out your personal wishes other than the legal ones. This is important and can be your spouse or partner, your child, a good friend, a relative, a neighbor—someone you trust with your life.

The following list includes some of the questions that have been asked throughout the book, but we like to keep the important details together for ease in making crucial decisions and to make it easy for your family in certain circumstances. Take your time (well, not too much time, if you know what we mean). You don't have to do this all at once. You might find that these questions create other questions, so just do it at your own pace.

DNR — DO NOT RESUSCITATE?

_____

_____

AUTOPSY?

_____

_____

ORGAN AND/OR TISSUE DONATIONS?

_____

_____

WHICH ORGANS AND TISSUES?

_____

_____

WHERE? (ORGANIZATIONS, SCHOOLS, HOSPITALS, INDIVIDUALS):

_____

_____

BODY DONATION?

_____

_____

WHICH SCHOOL/HOSPITAL?

_____

_____

Remember: if you have noted on your driver's license that you are an organ donor, your family is not obligated to follow your wishes. Since this act saves so many people's lives and enables people to lead vastly better lives, we strongly suggest you discuss this issue extensively with your family if they are in any way waffling here. They can still have a viewing/visitation and a traditional or green burial, but you must speak with different organizations first to confirm which ones will accommodate this. In addition to saving the life of someone who is ill, organizations receiving donated organs sometimes pay for the cremation. Hence our recommendation to plan first.

BURIAL OR CREMATION?

_____

IF BURIAL, TRADITIONAL OR GREEN?

_____

IF YOU WANT A TRADITIONAL BURIAL—
FUNERAL HOME OR NOT? IF SO, WHICH ONE?

_____

OPEN OR CLOSED CASKET?

_____

EMBALMED?

_____

WHAT TO WEAR?

_____

BUDGET?

_____

COST OF THE COFFIN?

_____

MAUSOLEUM (ABOVE GROUND)?

_____

CEMENT LINER?

_____

WHERE TO BE BURIED?

_____

TOMBSTONE OR MARKER? (GIVE SPECIFICS LIKE KIND OF STONE,
SCULPTURAL DETAIL, AND TEXT):

_____

_____

DESIGNATE PALLBEARERS

_____

_____

In the case of a funeral with all the trimmings, there are no warranties, no returns, and no resale, so your loved ones will be thankful if you do this in advance. If you do, they will not have to make any tortured decisions or possibly live with guilt for the rest of their lives. If you can afford to pre-pay for your casket and/or cremation and don't plan on moving far away for your retirement, then consider getting this out of the way now.

IF YOU WANT CREMATION -
FUNERAL HOME OR NOT?

_____

WHAT TO WEAR?

_____

_____

WHAT KIND OF CONTAINER FOR THE ASHES?

_____

_____

WHERE TO KEEP THE ASHES?

_____

_____

MAUSOLEUM OR COLUMBARIUM?

_____

GRAVESITE?

_____

SCATTERING LOCATION/LOCATIONS?

_____

WHAT TYPE OF SERVICE?
CIVILIAN OR MILITARY?

_____

FAMILY ONLY OR FAMILY AND FRIENDS?

_____

_____

RELIGIOUS OR NOT?

_____

_____

SPECIAL REQUESTS?

_____

_____

MARKER OR URN?

_____

BUDGET?

_____

TYPE?

_____

_____

INSCRIPTION?

_____

_____

OBITUARY?

_____

_____

WHO WILL WRITE IT, OR DO YOU WANT TO WRITE YOUR OWN?

_____

_____

OBITUARY PLACEMENT?

_____

_____

WHO AND WHAT DO YOU WANT MENTIONED?

_____

_____

_____

_____

PICTURE OR NOT, AND IF SO, WHICH PHOTO?

_____

_____

FINANCIAL DONATIONS IN YOUR NAME? IF SO, WHERE?

_____

_____

_____

_____

Now is also a good a time to get your "house in order"! Create a safe storage place, preferably a fire-resistant container or storage unit, to keep the following items. Go through these periodically and make sure that you're up to date.

WILL (NAME AND CONTACT INFORMATION OF ATTORNEY, IF YOU USED ONE)

_____

_____

_____

SAFETY DEPOSIT BOX (LOCATION AND KEY)

_____

_____

BIRTH CERTIFICATE

_____

_____

VEHICLE TITLES, REGISTRATION, INSURANCE COMPANY

_____

_____

_____

_____

TAX RECORDS (NAME AND NUMBER OF ACCOUNTANT OR TAX ATTORNEY)

_____

_____

BANK STATEMENTS (OR BANK NAME AND TYPES OF ACCOUNTS)

_____

_____

_____

_____

SOCIAL SECURITY NUMBERS FOR YOU, YOUR SPOUSE,
AND ANY YOUNG CHILDREN

_____

_____

_____

_____

CREDIT CARD ACCOUNTS

_____

_____

_____

_____

INSURANCE RECORDS (LIFE, HOMEOWNERS, RENTERS, VEHICLE, PROPERTY, ETC.)

_____

_____

_____

_____

_____

_____

IRA'S

_____

_____

DIVORCE PAPERS

_____

_____

LOAN AGREEMENTS (OWING AND OWED, TO OR FROM FRIENDS, ETC.)

_____

_____

_____

_____

HOUSE AND PROPERTY RECORDS

_____

_____

MARRIAGE CERTIFICATES

_____

_____

MILITARY DISCHARGE PAPERS

_____

_____

PENSION RECORDS

_____

_____

WHO WILL OVERSEE THE CARRYING OUT OF MY PERSONAL WISHES?
(GIVE FIRST, SECOND, EVEN THIRD CHOICES)

_____

_____

_____

PERSONAL ITEMS YOU WANT TO BEQUEATH TO CERTAIN PEOPLE

_____

_____

_____

_____

_____

_____

_____

_____

_____

_____

_____

_____

_____

_____

_____

FINAL THOUGHTS:

_____
_____
_____
_____
_____
_____
_____
_____
_____
_____
_____
_____
_____
_____
_____
_____
_____
_____
_____
_____
_____
_____
_____
_____
_____
_____
_____
_____
_____
_____
_____
_____

FINAL THOUGHTS:

_____

_____

_____

_____

_____

_____

_____

_____

_____

_____

_____

_____

_____

_____

_____

_____

_____

_____

_____

_____

_____

_____

_____

_____

_____

_____

_____

_____

_____

_____

_____

_____

_____

FINAL THOUGHTS:

_____

_____

_____

_____

_____

_____

_____

_____

_____

_____

_____

_____

_____

_____

_____

_____

_____

_____

_____

_____

_____

_____

_____

_____

_____

_____

_____

_____

_____

_____

_____

_____

_____

_____

_____

Now, congratulate yourself for everything you've done! Even if there are only a few things that you've completed in this book so far, build on it and be proud of what you have done. It's remarkable you've addressed this issue, even if only in a small way. It will bring you and your family peace of mind in the days ahead, and that's priceless.

By reading and working with this book, you have not only taken care of some important business, but you have also taken a step towards accepting your own mortality. According to psychiatrists, fear of death is the greatest fear of all (okay, maybe after public speaking), and it is the root of many of our neuroses—even though it's the one inevitable event of all of our lives.

So, if you've done some planning via this book for your grand finale, then you can honestly say that in some small way you've faced death and (hopefully) laughed out loud while doing so. How many people can say they've done that?

See you on the other side!

ABOUT
THE AUTHORS

Carmen Flowers was born and raised in North Carolina. She started her career as a professional commercial actress and voice-over talent in New York in the 1980s. She was equally interested in both sides of the camera and the microphone, so she opened an audio postproduction studio in midtown Manhattan, working with clients such as HBO, NBC, Comedy Central, J. Walter Thompson, and CBS. After selling the company, Carmen worked as an executive producer of commercials and independent features before forming her current media content development company, Little Black Dog Inc. She now happily splits her time between New York and her home in a small town in Maine, where she raises chickens, grows vegetables and flowers, writes, and enjoys the company of her favorite husband, Vern, and her little black pug, Duke Ellington.

Sue Bailey was born in Oregon, "grew up" in New York City, arriving as a teen to attend Cooper Union and study fine arts. She is one of five kids, two parents, and several important pet-kids. While presently happily unmarried, she is still looking in a very lazy way. Sue had spent her entire adult life at HBO mostly as a vice president promoting and working on some of the best TV shows ever created—but she is now working on her own projects full-time. She can honestly say that she has no fear of death—which is not to say she doesn't dislike the idea of any physical suffering on the way there. Intensely spiritual, she knows there is no "death"—just a transformation from one form to another. She actually looks forward to passing over and feeling the immensity and unfettered love of the soul. But in the meantime, she is cramming a lot of living and learning into those very few years on the Earth—mostly in her beloved New York.

ABOUT
CIDER MILL PRESS

Good ideas ripen with time. From seed to harvest, Cider Mill Press strives to bring fine reading, information, and entertainment together between the covers of its creatively crafted books. Our Cider Mill bears fruit twice a year, publishing a new crop of titles each Spring and Fall.

Visit us on the web at
www.cidermillpress.com
or write to us at
12 Port Farm Road
Kennebunkport, Maine 04046